Principles of Evidence for Policing

James Euale
Dianne Martin
Nora Rock
Jillan Sadek

1998

EMOND MONTGOMERY PUBLICATIONS LIMITED

TORONTO, CANADA

Emond Montgomery Publications Limited
60 Shaftesbury Avenue
Toronto ON M4T 1A3
http://www.emp.ca

Printed in Canada.

Edited, designed, and typeset by WordsWorth Communications, Toronto.
Cover design by Susan Darrach, Darrach Design.

We acknowledge the financial support of the Government of Canada through the Book Publishing Industry Development Program (BPIDP) for our publishing activities.

Canadian Cataloguing in Publication Data

Main entry under title:

Principles of evidence for policing

(Police foundations program)
Includes bibliographical references.
ISBN 978-1-55239-044-3

1. Evidence, Criminal—Canada.   I. Euale, James, 1947– . II. Series.

KE9312.P74 1998   345.71′06′0243632   C98-932954-2
KF9600.P74 1998

Contents

Preface   ix

About the Authors   xi

■ *Part* I   THE FUNDAMENTALS OF CRIMINAL EVIDENCE   1

CHAPTER 1   PROOF: INTRODUCTORY CONCEPTS   3

Proving the Offence   3

The Law of Evidence   6

Burden of Proof   8

Standard of Proof   10

Key Terms   12

Review   12

CHAPTER 2   GOOD EVIDENCE: RELEVANCE, MATERIALITY, AND PROBATIVE VALUE   17

Relevance and Materiality   17

Direct Versus Circumstantial Evidence   19

Probative Value   20

Corroborative Evidence   21

"Clean" Evidence   22

Key Terms   24

Review   24

CHAPTER 3   INADMISSIBILITY AND FACTORS THAT WEAKEN EVIDENCE   29

Prejudice   29

Hearsay   30

Opinion Evidence   36

Character Evidence   39

Privilege   42

Improperly Obtained Evidence   43

Key Terms   44

Review   45

CHAPTER 4   THE BLOODY GLOVE: PHYSICAL AND DOCUMENTARY EVIDENCE   51

Physical Evidence   51

Documentary Evidence   54

Key Terms   56

Review   56

CHAPTER 5   ORAL EVIDENCE AND WITNESSES   61

Competence   61

Compellability   63

Privilege   64

Experts   67

Prior Statements   69

The Mechanics of Testifying   72

Answering Questions   73

Key Terms   74

Review   75

CHAPTER 6   LEGAL RIGHTS OF WITNESSES AND OF THE ACCUSED, AND THE IMPLICATIONS FOR ADMISSIBILITY   79

Questioning Witnesses' Evidence Without Infringing the Rights of Witnesses   79

When Does a Witness Become a Suspect or an Accused?   80

Detention and Arrest   81

Charter Rights of Suspects and Accused   81

Exclusion of Evidence Collected in Violation of Rights   83

Key Terms   86

Review   86

CHAPTER 7

RESPECTING RIGHTS IN THE COLLECTION OF EVIDENCE: SEARCHES, WARRANTS, AND WIRETAPS   91

Searches   91

Warrantless Searches   91

Warrants   95

Wiretapping   99

Key Terms   101

Review   101

CHAPTER 8

INTERVIEWS, STATEMENTS, AND CONFESSIONS   105

Interviewing the Accused   105

Confessions   105

The Importance of Voluntariness   107

Key Terms   109

Review   109

CHAPTER 9

DISCLOSURE OBLIGATIONS   113

Disclosure   113

Key Terms   116

Review   117

CHAPTER 10

EVIDENCE SKILLS FOR POLICE   121

Taking Notes That Will Hold Up in Court   121

Tips for Giving Testimony   122

Key Terms   124

Review   124

■ *Part* II   **AN INTRODUCTION TO FORENSIC SCIENCE
                    AND THE COLLECTION OF PHYSICAL EVIDENCE   127**

CHAPTER 11   **THE PRESERVATION, COLLECTION, AND CONTINUITY OF
                PHYSICAL EVIDENCE   129**

                Introduction   129

                The Preservation of Evidence and the Crime Scene   130

                Security and Continuity of Possession   131

                The Introduction of Evidence Into Court   136

                Key Terms   138

                Review   139

CHAPTER 12   **PHYSICAL EVIDENCE AND EVIDENTIARY VALUE   147**

                Introduction   147

                Imprints and Impressions   147

                Writings and Documents   152

                Trace Elements   152

                Bodily Fluids: Blood, Semen, and Urine   153

                DNA Testing   154

                Gunshot Residue   155

                Firearm and Projectile Examination   156

                Bite Marks   156

                Broken Nails   157

                Fracture Matches   157

                Glass   157

                Key Terms   157

                Review   158

CHAPTER 13   **THE INVESTIGATION OF SUDDEN DEATH   163**

                Introduction   163

                The Chronology of Assumptions   163

                Evidence Indicating Homicide   164

                Evidence Indicating Suicide   165

Questions To Be Answered by the Investigation   166

Conclusion   170

Key Terms   171

Review   171

APPENDIX   RCMP INVESTIGATOR'S GUIDE TO FORENSIC EVIDENCE, SECOND EDITION   179

GLOSSARY OF TERMS   219

REFERENCES   227

Preface

For most people, the police function that comes most readily to mind is public protection—the police are there to keep us safe. But while crime prevention is a critical goal for our police forces, the reality is that most crimes are difficult to anticipate, and the police are most frequently called in to "pick up the pieces" after a crime has occurred. As a result, the gathering of evidence, sometimes a tedious process, emerges as a common and important job function for police officers at all levels of experience and training.

Although evidence collection, especially for novice officers, consists mostly of routine tasks such as note taking, careful attention to these tasks is essential to the prosecution and conviction of offenders, which in turn supports the most important preventive tool in the police arsenal: deterrence. By demonstrating their ability to identify and support the conviction of lawbreakers, the police establish their credibility and effectiveness, bringing them closer to their goals of crime prevention and the promotion of public safety. Every police officer, from the new recruit to the senior investigator, has the opportunity to make his or her contribution to these goals through the careful collection and preservation of evidence. The value of each individual contribution depends on an understanding of the role of evidence in a criminal prosecution.

This book provides police science students with a basic working knowledge of two important disciplines: law and forensic science. In describing the factors that make evidence more or less valuable for the prosecution, this book helps inform the developing judgment of novice "evidence collectors," assisting them in identifying opportunities to support the case against an accused, and to avoid any pitfalls that might weaken an otherwise promising investigation.

Part I of the book provides an introduction to trial evidence, with a focus on such issues as admissibility and reliability of evidence. Although almost anyone can collect evidence, collecting evidence that is free of taint due to coercion, mishandling, or sloppy procedures requires good judgment and a solid understanding of fundamental legal principles. On completion of this part, the student will understand the importance of collecting evidence systematically and in a way that is respectful of the rights of witnesses and the accused.

Part II introduces the student to the collection and preservation of physical evidence, and to some basic principles of forensic science. Although it is unlikely that a novice police officer will be required to undertake the systematic collection of physical evidence in a serious crime, it is important for all officers to have a working knowledge of the evidentiary potential of a crime scene, if only to create an awareness of how to avoid contaminating the evidence available. This part also underscores the importance of continuity and the maintenance of careful records with respect to evidentiary exhibits, laying a foundation for attentiveness to the recordkeeping tasks that protect collected evidence from legal challenges.

A new police recruit will likely have many years to wait before becoming involved in, for example, the collection of physical clues at a homicide scene, or the taking of an accused's confession; but it is never too early to begin bringing keen instincts and solid work habits to even the simplest evidence-gathering tasks. We hope that this book, a truly collaborative effort on the part of authors from diverse but complementary backgrounds, will assist in the development of those work skills, and will serve as the authors' own contribution to a dynamic police force and a safer society.

Nora Rock
December 1998

About the Authors

James Euale teaches in the Police Foundations Program at Sault college. His 25 years of experience with the RCMP, including several years with joint forces units (working with various police forces), brought a valuable real-world perspective to both the legal and forensic science components of the book.

Dianne Martin is a law professor at Osgoode Hall Law School at York University. She contributed both practical legal experience and an enduring interest in the issues at the heart of criminal law and evidence.

Nora Rock is an Ontario lawyer, working as an acquisitions editor at Emond Montgomery Publications. She brought her growing understanding of the unique educational needs of Police Foundations students to the task of coordinating this multiauthored work.

Jillan Sadek was a law student at Osgoode Hall Law School at York University when she worked on this book. She developed a first draft of much of the material, and her solid contribution made the remaining work a pleasure.

PART I

The Fundamentals of Criminal Evidence

CHAPTER 1
Proof: Introductory Concepts

CHAPTER OBJECTIVES

After completing this chapter, you should be able to:

◆ Explain the role of proof in a criminal case.

◆ Define "evidence" and list three types.

◆ Explain the role of evidence law and the roles of judge, jury, and counsel with respect to the evidence.

◆ Define and understand the concept of burden of proof.

◆ Define and understand the concept of standard of proof.

PROVING THE OFFENCE

Evidence law is the law of proof. Proof is an essential legal concept. To avoid convicting innocent people, the justice system cannot impose a penalty (a sentence) on an accused person unless there is convincing proof that the person is guilty of the offence charged.

For a suspect to be convicted of an offence, the offence must be *proved* in court. Enforcement personnel charge a suspect with a particular offence (or offences), and then it's up to the prosecution (the Crown) to *prove* the offence and answer any defences, so that the judge or jury is persuaded of the suspect's guilt. The suspect (who, once charged, is called the **accused**) can be convicted and sentenced only if the prosecution can successfully prove the offence.

accused
a suspect who has been charged with a crime

Acts

To prove an offence, the prosecution is required to prove certain acts or actions on which the offence is based. Many of these acts are described in the wording of the statute that creates the offence. For example, the *Criminal Code* describes the offence of robbery as follows:

> **Robbery**
> 343. Every one commits robbery who
> (a) steals, and for the purpose of extorting whatever is stolen or to prevent or overcome resistance to the stealing, uses violence or threats of violence to a person or property;

> (b) steals from any person and, at the time he steals or imme-
> diately before or immediately thereafter, wounds, beats, strikes
> or uses any personal violence to that person;
>
> (c) assaults any person with intent to steal from him; or
>
> (d) steals from any person while armed with an offensive
> weapon or imitation thereof.

In reading this description of robbery, it becomes clear that there are four ways to commit the offence. For each, it is possible to list the acts that the prosecution will have to prove.

In situation (a),

1. someone *has stolen* something, and

2. in stealing, that person *has used violence* or threats of violence to a person or property.

In situation (b),

1. someone *has stolen* something from another person, and

2. at or very near the time of stealing, the accused *has used "any personal violence"* to the victim.

In situation (c),

1. someone *has assaulted* another person.

   (In this situation, it is not necessary to prove that anything has actually been stolen. The only *act* that needs to be proved is an assault, but the assault must be accompanied by an intent to steal.)

In situation (d),

1. someone *has stolen* something from another person, and

2. while stealing, the alleged robber *was armed* with an offensive weapon or an imitation of one.

   Although most of the key acts that the prosecution will need to prove can be found in the words describing the offence, there may be others that cannot. A very common and important example is the *identity* of the accused.

Intent

In addition to proving acts or actions, all true crimes also require the prosecution to prove certain things about the accused's state of mind at the time of the offence. This aspect of proof is often referred to as **intent** or *mens rea*. Thus in the above robbery example, situation (c) depends on proof of a particular intent:

intent
sometimes called mens rea; *the mental element of an offence that must be proved to secure a conviction*

> 343. Every one commits robbery who ...
>
> (c) assaults any person with intent to steal from him ...

To prove robbery committed in this way, the Crown must prove

1. that the accused *has committed an assault* (an action), and

2. that the accused committed the assault *with intent to steal* from the victim (an intent).

In all four robbery situations, however, the prosecution has to prove that the conduct was intentional (that the accused had a "general" intent).

Together, the acts and intentions that the prosecution has to prove are known as the "essential elements" of an offence.

Evidence

The term **evidence** is a synonym for "proof" and has come to describe the information presented before the court by the prosecution and the defence in their efforts to prove the facts that will establish the actions and intentions (or lack of either) necessary to prove or defend against the offences charged.

evidence
any information or physical material relied upon in legal proceedings to prove or disprove a fact or legal argument

Evidence can take many forms, including:

1. **Oral testimony** of witnesses, sometimes called *viva voce* **evidence**. This is information delivered by witnesses who testify in court in response to questions from the prosecution and the defence.

oral testimony/ *viva voce* evidence
the spoken (verbal) evidence of a witness as given under oath or affirmation in a legal proceeding

2. *Physical objects* (usually called "real evidence") become "exhibits" once they form part of the **trial record** (the written record of the court proceedings). Examples can include an alleged murder weapon, photographs of a crime scene, and a sample of an illicit substance recovered from a suspect. The science of **forensics** deals with the collection, preservation, and study of this kind of evidence.

trial record
the official written transcript of a legal proceeding

forensics
a discipline based on the collection and study of scientific information that is destined for use in legal proceedings

3. **Documentary evidence** (which, like real evidence, becomes an exhibit or exhibits when introduced in court). This is evidence contained in written documents such as business records, transcripts of recorded conversations, and affidavits (written records of witness evidence).

documentary evidence
a class of physical/real evidence that consists of documents of any kind, handwritten or mechanically produced

Some kinds of evidence are difficult to classify. For example, a ransom note in a kidnapping case may be physical evidence for some purposes and documentary evidence for others.

Facts

In legal cases, "facts" are what a court has decided are the facts, based on the evidence presented. Nothing is a "fact" until a judge or jury has decided that it is. Because our system is *adversarial*, with both sides presenting evidence, a court will often hear more than one version of an event or interpretation of information. The judge or jury decides which witnesses to believe and which version is preferable.

SUMMARY

1. Before a person can be convicted and sentenced, the offence must be proved in court.

2. To prove an offence, the prosecution has to introduce evidence to establish the "essential elements" of the offence. These usually are

   a. acts or actions, and

   b. intent or *mens rea*.

3. Legal proof is called evidence. The types of evidence include

   a. oral testimony,

   b. physical evidence, and

   c. documentary evidence.

THE LAW OF EVIDENCE

The law of evidence is the set of legal rules that governs the collection of evidence and the presentation of evidence to the court for consideration.

Admissibility

Not all of the evidence available to parties to a hearing will be admissible in court. Among the reasons the court may have for declining to admit a piece of evidence are the following:

1. The evidence is irrelevant or immaterial to the issues to be decided—it doesn't relate to or doesn't help to prove any fact that needs to be proved.

2. The evidence, by its nature, may be unreliable. For example, it may be **hearsay** (secondhand) evidence. The court will normally admit hearsay only when there is no firsthand evidence.

hearsay
evidence that is indirect in that it is being given by a witness who has heard it from another source; second-hand evidence

3. The *prejudicial* quality of the evidence (its tendency to influence decision makers in a way that is unfair or undeserved) outweighs its *probative value* (its tendency to prove or disprove an important fact).

4. The evidence was obtained in a way that was *unfair* to the accused or *violated his or her rights* under the *Canadian Charter of Rights and Freedoms* or other legislation (this is why extreme care is required in collecting evidence and handling suspects and witnesses).

5. Because of procedural rules or for other reasons, admitting the evidence would be unfair to the defence or would waste time or confuse the issues. For example, if the prosecution holds back some evidence and attempts to call it only after the defence has finished calling its evidence, this is called "splitting the case" and is not permitted.

The Players in a Criminal Trial

The Judge

The task of deciding whether a piece of evidence will not be admitted in court belongs primarily to the judge, who is guided by the rules of evidence and, in the many cases where the rules allow room for interpretation, his or her discretion. Deciding on the admissibility of evidence is one of the most important parts of the judge's job, especially when there is a jury, because improper decisions about the admissibility of evidence can lead to a verdict being overturned (changed) if the losing side successfully appeals.

In a trial by judge alone, the judge is also the **trier of fact**. He or she is responsible for applying the law, for deciding whether the facts meet the legal requirements (by applying the *standard of proof*), and for issuing a verdict based on the evidence.

When there is a jury, the judge is responsible for **charging the jury**. In a statement to the jury at the end of the trial, the judge reviews the legal requirements of the case (as he or she has interpreted them), explains the relevant rules of evidence and the standard of proof, and describes the decision or decisions that the jury must make to come to its verdict.

trier of fact
the decision maker(s) charged with determining whether the necessary facts of a case have been proved—the jury in a jury trial, or the judge in a trial by judge alone

charging the jury
the judge's instructions to the jury, usually at the end of a trial, in preparation for the jury's deliberations

The Jury

In a trial by judge and jury, the jurors are the triers of fact. They issue a verdict based on the evidence, with help from the judge's charge and his or her instructions throughout the trial. There is never a jury without a judge, because the judge is still needed to interpret the legal requirements.

Counsel

Counsel (lawyers) for the prosecution and for the defence also have a role to play in enforcing the rules of evidence. As the evidence is being presented in court, each lawyer listens carefully to ensure that the judge does not admit any evidence that would be damaging to the lawyer's case and that might be inadmissible. When the other side tries to introduce such evidence and the judge doesn't intervene to exclude it, counsel will often argue for exclusion by making an **objection**. It's then up to the judge to consider whether the objection is valid, often after hearing *submissions* (argument) from the other side. If the objection is valid, the judge will say that it is *sustained*. If the objection is invalid, the judge will say that it is *overruled*. Because evidence is not a science and the rules are open to interpretation, knowing when to object and what objections to make are important skills that lawyers develop through experience.

objection
a request that evidence about to be given be ruled inadmissible (by the judge)

Witnesses

Witnesses are people who testify (speak) in court in response to questions from counsel. They are called to give evidence because they have

witness
in a court case, any person who is called before the court to give evidence under oath or affirmation

information about the case or can provide an expert opinion on an issue. Their testimony becomes part of the *trial record* of evidence. In some cases the accused gives evidence, and thus becomes a witness for the defence.

SUMMARY

1. Evidence law is the set of rules governing the collection and presentation of evidence.

2. Not all evidence is admissible in court. Reasons for excluding evidence include irrelevance, immateriality, unreliability, undue prejudice, problems with collection of the evidence, and unfairness to the other side.

3. The judge is primarily responsible for controlling the admission of evidence, but counsel assist by arguing for or against the admission of evidence.

4. In a trial by judge alone, the judge is the trier of fact. In a trial by judge and jury, the jurors are the triers of fact.

5. Witnesses are people who give evidence in court. The accused can be a witness.

BURDEN OF PROOF

Definition

burden of proof
the requirement of proving a particular fact or argument; the onus

The term "burden of proof" is used to identify which person or party is responsible for proving a particular fact, issue, or case. If a party is responsible for proving something, he or she is said to have the **burden of proof**. In our adversarial system, the side that makes the allegation (or claim or accusation) has to prove it, while the other side always has the right to answer the accusation, in open court, in front of a fair and impartial judge or judge and jury.

Hockey Puck or Hot Potato?

Holding the burden of proof in a legal case is like having the puck in a hockey game, for the holder changes from time to time. Because the actions of one side can cause the burden of proof to shift, controlling who has the burden at a particular time or with respect to a particular issue can become a matter of strategy.

For example, in almost all offences it's up to the prosecution to prove the elements of the offence. But in some cases, once the prosecution has proved a particular fact, the burden shifts to the defence:

Possession [of] ... Counterfeit Money

450. Every one who, without lawful justification or excuse, the proof of which lies on him ...

    (b) has in his custody or possession ...

counterfeit money is guilty of an indictable offence and liable to imprisonment for a term not exceeding fourteen years.

Where the offence of possession of counterfeit money is concerned, once the prosecution has proved the fact of possession—that the accused has the money in his or her custody or possession—the offence is successfully proved, unless the accused can prove that he or she had lawful justification or excuse ("the proof ... lies on him").

In general, it is easier *not* to have the burden of proof (and the responsibility for gathering and presenting evidence). From this perspective, the burden is less like a hockey puck and more like a hot potato.

A "Layered" Concept

Though the notion of burden of proof is simple enough, tracking the burden of proof as a case unfolds is more complicated. Burden of proof is a "layered" concept, in the sense that both parties can hold the burden during the trial, but for different purposes.

Proving the Case

Our entire criminal justice system is founded on the belief that a person is *innocent until proven guilty*.

Implied in this belief is the prosecution's responsibility for proving the accused's guilt. As far as the case in its broadest sense is concerned, the burden of proof *always* lies with the prosecution. The accused is not even required to defend himself or herself, but can sit silently by, hoping that the prosecution will fail to prove its case.

Proving a Defence

Defending the charge may involve asking questions or calling witnesses to raise a reasonable doubt on a material point. Less often, the accused will actually have to prove the defence. Take, for example, an accused charged with murder. The prosecution may have the burden of proving that he or she (1) caused the death of a human being and (2) *meant* to do it:

Murder

229. Culpable homicide is murder

    (a) where the person who causes the death of a human being

        (i) means to cause his death. ...

If the defence is that the accused caused the death, but that he or she acted in self-defence, then to be acquitted the accused only needs to raise a reasonable doubt that he or she acted in self-defence. This is the usual situation. The exception is a defence based on mental illness. If the accused chooses to assert a defence of *mental disorder* (insanity), he or she has the burden of proving that, at the time death was caused, he or she was suffering from a mental disorder that affected his or her reasoning in a specific way (a fact):

> **Defence of Mental Disorder**
>
> 16.(1) No person is criminally responsible for an act committed or an omission made while suffering from a mental disorder that rendered the person incapable of appreciating the nature and quality of the act or omission or of knowing that it was wrong.

In this example, although the prosecution has the ultimate burden of proof in the trial, the accused has the burden of proving the defence.

Proving the Facts

As explained above, the court cannot merely accept the facts as alleged by either party—in order to rely on a particular fact, a party must *prove* it. At this level of evidence, each party has the burden of proving the facts on which it is relying in its efforts to substantiate an offence or assert a defence.

SUMMARY

1. The burden of proof is the responsibility for proving something.

2. The burden of proving the offence or offences in a criminal trial always lies with the prosecution.

3. The burden of proof with respect to particular issues and facts can shift throughout the course of a trial.

STANDARD OF PROOF

Definition

The term "standard of proof" refers to the degree to which the judge or jury must be persuaded. In everyday matters we make decisions based on varying degrees of certainty, depending on how important the question is. For example, how certain do you have to be that it will rain before you decide to take an umbrella with you when you go out? What "evidence" persuades you?

standard of proof
the degree of certainty of the truth of a fact required before that fact can be relied on in support of a particular verdict or legal decision

Legal questions are similar. The **standard of proof** is the answer to the question, How convinced does law require me (or the trier of fact) to be?

Two Standards

There are two recognized standards of proof:

1. proof on a balance of probabilities, and

2. proof beyond a reasonable doubt.

Balance of Probabilities

Proof on a balance of probabilities, sometimes called the civil standard of proof, requires that the evidence be sufficient to convince the trier of fact that the fact at issue is *more likely than not* to be true.

In other words, if, after hearing evidence in support of a fact, the jury is 51 percent convinced that the fact is true, the fact has been proved on a balance of probabilities.

In a civil (non-criminal) case, the required standard of proof for the *whole case* is the balance of probabilities. If the plaintiff (the party who started the lawsuit) can prove his or her side of the story (the claim) on a balance of probabilities, he or she wins the case.

proof on a balance of probabilities
proof that leaves the trier of fact at least 51 percent certain of the truth of a fact

Beyond a Reasonable Doubt

Where **proof beyond a reasonable doubt** is the required standard of proof, the evidence must be sufficient to convince the trier of fact with reasonable certainty that the fact at issue is true.

Proof beyond a reasonable doubt is the required standard of proof for criminal offences. For an accused to be convicted, the trier of fact must be convinced of his or her guilt beyond a reasonable doubt. This is a much more stringent standard than the one required in civil cases. The reason for this is obvious—a criminal conviction can carry serious penalties (such as incarceration) and the justice system recognizes the need to be very certain of an accused's guilt before subjecting him or her to a deprivation of liberty or other serious sanctions.

proof beyond a reasonable doubt
proof that is convincing beyond any doubt that a reasonable person could formulate

Standard Within a Standard

The standard of proof in criminal cases is complicated by the fact that although the criminal standard of proof is proof beyond a reasonable doubt, the individual pieces of evidence that support the elements of the offence are generally considered to be subject to the less onerous civil standard. Unless they constitute elements of the offence (key facts without which the offence cannot be established), these pieces of evidence need only be proved on a balance of probabilities. Why? Because it can be argued that although some facts may not be proved true beyond a reasonable doubt, the evidence may be convincing enough *as a whole* to eliminate reasonable doubts from the mind of the trier of fact.

SUMMARY

1. Standard of proof means the degree of certainty that the trier of fact is required to have before accepting a fact or an offence as proved.

2. There are two standards of proof:

   a. on a balance of probabilities (the civil standard), and

   b. beyond a reasonable doubt (the criminal standard).

3. In a criminal case, individual pieces of evidence that support the key facts of an offence need only be proved on a balance of probabilities.

KEY TERMS

accused	trier of fact
intent	charging the jury
evidence	objection
oral testimony/*viva voce* evidence	witness
trial record	burden of proof
forensics	standard of proof
documentary evidence	proof on a balance of probabilities
hearsay	proof beyond a reasonable doubt

REVIEW

■ TRUE OR FALSE?

_____ 1. It's up to the accused person to prove that he or she didn't commit the offence charged.

_____ 2. The accused's state of mind while committing the offence is always irrelevant to his or her guilt.

_____ 3. "Evidence" can include witness testimony, physical objects, and documents.

_____ 4. The Crown ultimately decides which evidence is admissible in court.

_____ 5. The manner in which evidence is collected can affect its admissibility.

_____ 6. Evidence that is irrelevant is not admissible in court.

_____ 7. When a judge agrees with an objection from counsel, the objection is sustained.

_____ 8. The standard of proof describes which side is responsible for proving that the offence occurred.

_____ 9. A criminal case can be tried by a judge, a judge and jury, or a jury alone.

_____ 10. A criminal offence must be proved beyond a reasonable doubt before a sentence can be imposed.

■ MULTIPLE CHOICE

1. An accused is said to be innocent until proven guilty because

   a. the prosecution has the burden of proof

   b. the accused can't be convicted without proof

   c. the standard of proof must be met before a conviction can be entered

   d. all of the above

2. The party or parties with final control over the admission of evidence is or are

   a. the judge

   b. the jury

   c. the judge and the jury

   d. counsel for the prosecution

3. The following is *not* a reason for excluding evidence:

   a. the evidence is immaterial

   b. the evidence might cause undue prejudice

   c. the evidence is *viva voce*

   d. the evidence was collected in violation of the accused's rights

4. The criminal standard of proof is "beyond a reasonable doubt" because

   a. the justice system must be very certain of guilt before subjecting an accused to criminal sanctions

   b. if there's enough reason to arrest an accused, there can be little doubt of the accused's guilt

   c. before convicting, the trier of fact must be at least 51 percent certain that the accused committed the offence

   d. in a criminal trial, no amount of doubt is unreasonable

■ FILL IN THE BLANKS

1. Once enforcement personnel have charged an accused with an offence, it's up to the _____ to prove that the offence was committed.

2. A bloody glove is an example of _____ evidence.

3. Evidence may be excluded when its prejudicial quality outweighs its _____ value.

4. Two different standards of proof are proof _____ and proof beyond a reasonable doubt.

■ SHORT ANSWER

1. After reading the following section of the *Criminal Code,* list the acts or intentions that the prosecution may have to prove to get a conviction.

Cheating at Play

   209. Every one who, with intent to defraud any person, cheats while playing a game or in holding the stakes for a game or in betting is guilty of an indictable offence and liable to imprisonment for a term not exceeding two years.

2. List three reasons a judge might have for excluding a piece of evidence sought to be presented in court.

3. Describe the role of counsel in influencing the admission of evidence.

4. Describe a situation in which the burden of proof lies with the defence.

5. Compare the civil "balance of probabilities" and criminal "beyond a reasonable doubt" standards of proof.

CHAPTER 2

Good Evidence: Relevance, Materiality, and Probative Value

CHAPTER OBJECTIVES

After completing this chapter, you should be able to:

◆ Explain the difference between relevant and material evidence.

◆ Discuss what would make a piece of evidence more or less likely to be admitted in court.

◆ Define and understand circumstantial evidence.

◆ Explain what the concept of continuity involves.

◆ Discuss the meaning of the term "corroborative evidence."

Not all evidence is created equal. Like building blocks, different pieces of evidence can be weak or strong depending on their characteristics. To prove its case, the prosecution wants to build the strongest wall of evidence possible against an accused person. The strength of this wall depends on the constituent pieces of evidence being the best available. Relevance, materiality, probative value, and corroboration are the characteristics of strong evidence.

RELEVANCE AND MATERIALITY

As was stated in chapter 1, not all of the evidence available to the defence or the prosecution will be admissible in court. For example, the court may refuse to admit evidence that is irrelevant or immaterial to the issues to be decided.

Materiality refers to the matters that the prosecution must establish to prove its case. Relevance refers to evidence that is related to the material issues in a way that tends to establish or "prove" those issues.

Relevance is the logical relationship that makes a proposition more or less probable. For example, given the statement, "Susie did not go to the store today because it was raining," the fact that it was raining is a

relevance
the tendency of a piece of evidence to prove or disprove a proposition

relevant explanation for why Susie was unable to go out. Conversely, given the statement, "Susie did not go to the store today because her sister, Julie, won the math prize," the fact that Susie's sister won the math prize is clearly not relevant to explaining why Susie did not go out.

Evidence is relevant when it tends to prove or disprove a proposition. Logic and common sense link the evidence to the proposition by means of generalizations. For example, to prove that the season is spring (the proposition), it is relevant to establish that roses are in bloom. The commonsense generalization is that roses bloom in spring, and thus the fact that they are in bloom is relevant to proving the season. However, relevance is rarely absolute—it can be challenged, and the link weakened. For example, one could ask *where* the roses are blooming—in a greenhouse? in Florida?

It is important to "unpack" the reasoning and identify the generalization that must be operating in order to establish the proposition, because this permits one to identify the limitations and weaknesses in the evidence. To prove that it is spring, a more persuasive generalization would be: "Early blooming roses bloom outdoors in Canada in the spring." This generalization also reveals that more evidence is needed to prove the season: the type of rose (early blooming) and where the roses are growing (outdoors, in Canada). However, as long as there is a reasonable level of relevance in a piece of evidence, it will usually be admissible. Further challenges to its weight or value as proof can be addressed in the course of legal argument.

Relevance is the most important factor in determining which pieces of evidence will be admitted in court. If something is not logically relevant, there is clearly no point in wasting the court's time by having lawyers argue about it during the trial. Thus, by admitting only relevant proof, the judge streamlines the use of court time and narrows the discussion to exactly what is needed to prove or disprove the propositions made by the prosecution and defence.

materiality
the degree to which a piece of evidence is necessary in proving a proposition

Materiality, on the other hand, refers to matters that one side must prove to win its point or the case. The law defines what must be proved in a particular case or criminal charge, but in many cases a point is very obvious or not in contention. In those circumstances, the other side can agree that there is no need to call witnesses or present evidence to prove the point—it is admitted. Courts always appreciate counsel who narrow the issues that must be proved to the questions that are truly contentious.

information
a form, prepared at the time of the laying of a charge, describing the offence(s) with which a suspect has been charged

In summary, material issues are largely defined by

1. How the parties have defined the case.

2. How the offence is defined in the *Criminal Code*.

indictment
a form, often prepared after a fuller investigation, setting out the offence(s) on which a conviction will be sought at trial

3. How the offence is defined in the **information** (the form that sets out what the accused person is charged with after he or she has been arrested) or in the **indictment** (the form that sets out what the accused person will be tried for at the trial).

Thus, not all evidence that may be relevant will also be material. Consider the example of a homicide case where the defence concedes the manner in which a stabbing victim was killed. The autopsy photos would likely not be material evidence, as it would be redundant to introduce photos of a knife wound when the defence had already admitted that the accused stabbed the victim. Materiality, however, is not always so easily defined. The prosecutor may argue, for example, that even if the cause of death is not a material fact in issue, the violent manner in which the deceased came to die is. Thus the autopsy photos are material to the issue of intent, showing anger and a "guilty mind," and should therefore be admissible.

Similarly, some statutes may not require that certain facts be proved in order to secure a conviction. For example, in absolute liability offences (also known as strict liability offences), it is not necessary to prove intent (or *mens rea*), so evidence of knowledge or lack of knowledge on the part of the perpetrator is *not* material evidence and therefore is inadmissible. Many quasi-criminal regulatory statutes, such as environmental statutes and the *Highway Traffic Act*, create strict and absolute liability offences (in contrast to true crimes, such as offences under the *Criminal Code* and the *Narcotic Control Act*). For example, if the accused is charged with possession of undersized fish, and defence counsel attempt to adduce evidence that the accused did not know that the fish were undersized, such evidence will not be admitted, because it is immaterial. Such evidence may rationally persuade the trier of fact of the accused's state of mind, but it is still immaterial, for Parliament and the courts have decided that there is no need to prove knowledge of the offence—it is sufficient that the forbidden action (possession of the fish) was committed.

SUMMARY

1. To be admitted, evidence must meet the requirements of relevance and materiality.

2. Evidence is relevant if it logically assists in proving an offence.

3. Evidence is material when it relates to a matter that must be proved in order to win the case.

DIRECT VERSUS CIRCUMSTANTIAL EVIDENCE

Direct evidence is evidence that establishes a material point without the need to rely on a generalization to support a logical inference. For example, if Bill confesses that he robbed a local convenience store, this is direct evidence that he committed the robbery. No inferences need be drawn if Bill confesses to the material elements of the crime.

In contrast, **circumstantial evidence** refers to proof that may logically support material facts. Proof is based on the judge or jury drawing an inference from these peripheral facts that the material facts are more

direct evidence
evidence that proves an important fact without the need to speculate

circumstantial evidence
evidence that logically supports a fact, but that is at least partly dependent on speculation

or less likely to have occurred (Delisle, 1996, p. 23). Certainly, circumstantial evidence may not cause the judge or jury to draw the conclusion that it is offered to establish, but it is relevant enough to be admissible if it logically leads the judge or jury to make that connection (Paciocco, 1996, p. 21). Thus if Bill does not confess to the robbery, but Pete, Bill's friend, saw him going toward the convenience store shortly before the robbery occurred, this may be circumstantial evidence that Bill committed the crime. That Bill was seen in the area logically supports the notion that he could have been at the convenience store at the material time. This evidence, through inferences, thus supports a material fact.

Another example of the difference between direct and circumstantial evidence comes from the evidence of eyewitnesses. If a witness is able to testify that she saw the accused strangle the deceased, her evidence is direct evidence of that material fact. However, if she is willing to testify only that she heard the deceased choking and moments later saw the accused standing over the body grinning, this is only circumstantial evidence of the accused having strangled the deceased (Delisle, 1996, p. 24).

SUMMARY

1. Direct evidence proves material facts.

2. Circumstantial evidence proves facts that are logically supportive of material facts.

PROBATIVE VALUE

probative value
the relative relevance and materiality ("proof power") of a particular piece of evidence

Another characteristic of strong evidence is its **probative value**—how far the evidence probes the heart of the matter (in other words, its "proof power"). For example, if the perpetrator of a crime is known to ride a yellow bike, and the accused is also known to ride a yellow bike, this is a fact that has some probative value, for it is relevant to identifying the perpetrator. However, a piece of evidence that would have more probative value with respect to identity would be fingerprints left at the scene by the perpetrator that matched the accused's. This evidence would be more helpful—or have a higher probative value—than bike colour in establishing the link between the perpetrator and the accused.

In deciding which pieces of evidence should be admitted, the judge needs to decide whether the benefits of the evidence outweigh the costs. Probative value is one way to measure the benefits of a piece of evidence or how important the evidence is in proving a chain of events. These benefits must be balanced against the costs of admitting the evidence—in other words, against the degree of **prejudice** that may result from the evidence being tendered. Prejudice is defined as how a piece of evidence may tend to mislead the trier and consequently be unfair to the accused. Defined another way, evidence that is prejudicial has a tendency to be given more weight by judge or jury than it deserves (Paciocco, 1996, p. 26).

prejudice
the undesirable "side effects" of a piece of (usually, inflammatory) evidence that may be deemed unfair to the accused

Probative Value	Versus	Prejudice
Proof power of the evidence		Impermissible reasoning, tendency to mislead

If the prejudice outweighs the probative value, the evidence is more likely to be excluded. For example, that an accused has a criminal record is often considered to have little or no probative value, but as it is definitely prejudicial it may be excluded. In 1988 the Supreme Court of Canada in *R v. Corbett* determined that a judge has the discretion to exclude the use of a prior criminal record unless the prosecution can prove particular relevance. Knowing that an accused has a criminal record may create a hostile and distorted impression about the accused, because the judge or jury may assume that if someone has broken the law once, he or she will be likely to break it again. This is called **propensity evidence**, which the Supreme Court considers to be impermissible reasoning. Clearly, this type of reasoning has little or no probative value, and much prejudicial effect. Judging a case based on the past character of the accused is discriminatory and unfairly puts the accused in a position where he or she is being judged for past wrongs instead of being properly tried, in an unbiased manner, on the evidence before the court.

propensity evidence
evidence that is tendered to prove the "propensity" of an accused to act in a particular way

SUMMARY

1. The probative value of evidence must outweigh its prejudicial effect for it to be admitted by the judge.

2. Reasoning that relies on someone's propensity to act in a certain manner is considered impermissible by the courts.

CORROBORATIVE EVIDENCE

Any independently sourced evidence that supports another piece of evidence or a proposition is called **corroborative evidence**. In a case of alleged sexual assault, for example, semen found on the victim's underwear that matches the accused's DNA may be evidence that corroborates the complaint.

corroborative evidence
independently sourced evidence that supports another piece of evidence

Formerly, some kinds of evidence were considered to be particularly unsafe and required corroborative evidence before they could be believed. Judges would warn juries of the dangers of convicting an accused person on the uncorroborated evidence of certain witnesses, namely children, accomplices to crime, and complainants alleging a sexual offence (Paciocco, 1996, p. 279). A number of the statutory corroboration requirements relating to certain witnesses have been repealed. Nevertheless, commonsense assumptions about who is providing the evidence give some evidence less weight. For example, where a friend of the accused who is charged with the same offence as the accused claims to have seen his friend rob a convenience store, his testimony may be less believable than that of the store owner, who has no obvious motive to lie. Clearly, in this case any independent evidence confirming the friend's version of events would assist in his being believed, but such evidence is not required by the courts. However, some statutory corroboration rules still apply. For example, s. 133 of the *Criminal Code* provides that no person can be convicted of perjury "on the evidence of only one witness unless the evidence of that witness is corroborated in a material particular by evidence that implicates the accused" (Paciocco, 1996, p. 279).

Generally, however, corroboration always helps to strengthen evidence and build a strong wall of proof. Especially when looking at a case from the prosecution's perspective, the case against an accused must be very strong to convince the judge or jury beyond a reasonable doubt. It is unlikely that a judge or jury will be convinced to such a degree without corroborative facts of some kind.

SUMMARY

1. Some statutory provisions prescribe the need for corroborative evidence before an offence can be proved.

2. Although the identity of some witnesses (children, co-accused, etc.) may raise doubts about the reliability of their evidence, there is no legal requirement that their evidence be corroborated.

3. In cases depending on one person's word against another's, it's usually helpful to have some corroborative evidence, but, again, corroborative evidence is not required by law.

"CLEAN" EVIDENCE

How evidence is gathered is extremely important, because improperly obtained evidence may be excluded in court. This applies as much to the gathering of physical items as it does to the taking of oral statements. These processes must be carried out scrupulously to avoid subsequent doubts about whether proper procedures were followed. Properly obtained evidence is strong or **"clean" evidence**.

"clean" evidence
physical evidence that is free of taint related to mishandling by investigators or prosecutors

Crime scene preservation is key when searching for physical evidence. Proper crime scene preservation permits a structured and thorough search and the seizure of as much physical evidence as possible. It also ensures the admissibility of seized physical evidence. All of this, in turn, helps to establish continuity. Continuity means that every physical object dealt with by the police since their arrival at the scene is tracked and accounted for. Consider a case where a bloodstained pillow is taken from a crime scene. To prove its case, the Crown must be able to call on, among others,

◆ the officer who found the pillow

◆ the person who numbered and recorded the pillow

◆   the officer who drove the pillow to the forensics lab

◆   the lab operator who analyzed the blood

◆   the officer who returned the pillow to the Crown's evidence repository to await trial.

All of these people may be required to testify to establish continuity.

This degree of care is necessary to demonstrate that the object presented in court did in fact come from the relevant location and that it was not tampered with or contaminated.

The first step in ensuring continuity is to ensure that no unauthorized persons have access to the crime scene. A crime scene cannot be examined for physical evidence until the site has been identified, its boundaries defined, and steps taken to protect it from contamination.

The standard evidence collection procedure for imprints and impressions is as follows:

1.   Record, measure, and photograph in place.

2.   Collect intact if the article on which the imprint or impression was made is not too large or heavy and can be transported without damaging the evidence.

3.   Dust and lift any fingerprints and make a cast of any impressions.

4.   Mark for identification and package carefully.

5.   Transport to laboratory.

6.   Protect the scene and any articles seized from contamination by any outside source. This is particularly important if DNA or other sensitive tests such as fibre analysis are likely.

Naturally, the types of evidence gathering that will be helpful in each case depend on the offence. For example, if the offence is drug trafficking, there is usually no need to look for bloodspatter patterns. In a trafficking case, as per s. 5(1) of the *Controlled Drugs and Substances Act*, one wants the drugs themselves (as physical evidence), the testimony of drug customers (as oral evidence), someone who will identify the accused, and so forth. The *Criminal Code* typically sets out what needs to be proved for each offence, and as such is a good guide to follow when in doubt about which pieces of evidence should be sought.

SUMMARY

1.   Obtaining clean evidence means preserving continuity and ensuring that proper procedures are followed.

2.   It is important that the evidence be properly obtained. Otherwise, the judge may exclude it at trial.

KEY TERMS

relevance	probative value
materiality	prejudice
information	propensity evidence
indictment	corroborative evidence
direct evidence	"clean" evidence
circumstantial evidence	

REVIEW

■ TRUE OR FALSE?

_____ **1.** Some *Criminal Code* offences require corroborative evidence.

_____ **2.** If someone is an eyewitness to a stabbing, his or her testimony constitutes circumstantial evidence of the offence.

_____ **3.** If an accused has a criminal record, it is possible that this information will not be admitted in court, for fear of its prejudicial effect.

_____ **4.** For evidence to be relevant it must also be material.

_____ **5.** Continuity is disturbed if no one can prove who drove the sample to the lab.

_____ **6.** If the statute specifies that intent is not an issue, the accused's knowledge may still be material evidence.

_____ **7.** A complainant's statement is direct evidence of an offence.

_____ **8.** A child's testimony can never be believed without corroboration.

_____ **9.** If evidence is not relevant it will never be admitted.

_____ **10.** If the prejudicial effect of a piece of evidence outweighs its probative value it may still be admitted.

■ MULTIPLE CHOICE

1. Direct evidence differs from circumstantial evidence because

    a. direct evidence is always testimonial

    b. direct evidence does not need corroboration

    c. direct evidence proves facts directly, without the need for speculation

    d. direct evidence is obtained properly

2. The judge may decide not to admit evidence because

    a. the accused already has a criminal record

    b. the evidence's prejudicial effect outweighs its probative value

    c. the evidence lacks corroboration

    d. the evidence supports only circumstantial facts

3. Probative value refers to

    a. the degree of directness of the evidence

    b. how important a piece of evidence is in logically proving a case

    c. the lack of prejudice attached to a piece of evidence

    d. whether a generalization can prove a proposition

4. Prejudicial evidence is usually not admitted because

    a. it does not possess enough probative value

    b. it may mislead the judge or jury

    c. it generally reflects impermissible reasoning

    d. all of the above

■ SHORT ANSWER

1. Explain the difference between relevant and material evidence.

2. If an accused was seen in the area where a crime occurred, would this be circumstantial or direct evidence? Why?

3. If Margie is a victim of sexual assault, is it relevant that she is a
    prostitute? Why?

4. Do some kinds of evidence need corroboration more than others? If
    so, which kinds?

5. How does one ensure that evidence, if relevant and admissible, will not be excluded because it was improperly obtained?

CHAPTER 3

Inadmissibility and Factors That Weaken Evidence

CHAPTER OBJECTIVES

After completing this chapter, you should be able to:

◆ Define the concept of hearsay.

◆ Discuss the exceptions to the hearsay rule.

◆ Discuss the rules surrounding opinion evidence.

◆ Explain when evidence of someone's character is admissible.

◆ Define privilege.

◆ Explain why some evidence may be considered to be improperly obtained.

The general rule of evidence is that if it is relevant, it is admissible. However, there are exceptions to this rule designed to make trials fair and efficient.

In the previous chapter reference was made to several factors that may cause evidence to be inadmissible in a trial. Although the **admissibility** of evidence is important, the weight given to evidence is also crucial to distinguishing weak evidence from strong evidence. **Weight** refers to how reliable a piece of evidence is and how effectively it establishes a point. A very trustworthy piece of evidence will be heavily weighted, meaning the judge will put more emphasis on it and instruct the jury to do the same. Conversely, though another piece of evidence may be admitted, it may be given little weight because it lacks reliability. In this chapter we will examine more closely the rules that prohibit or restrict the use of such types of evidence. Even though there are general rules excluding certain types of evidence, however, there are also *exceptions*. Thus it is important to understand both the *exclusionary* rules and the exceptions to them.

admissibility
the likelihood of a piece of evidence to be allowed (by the judge) to be presented in a court case

weight
the probative value/importance assigned to a piece of evidence, based on an assessment of its reliability

PREJUDICE

One of the main factors that renders evidence less likely to be admitted is prejudice to the accused. As discussed in the previous chapter, prejudicial evidence refers to any evidence that is likely to mislead the judge or jury, or be unfairly detrimental to the accused. This fundamental concept of prejudicial evidence is rooted on our justice system's stress on two values: first, accuracy in fact finding, and second, the importance of the presumption of innocence and the value of a fair trial. It is important to reach the correct result in a trial, but that will not happen if the trier of fact is more influenced by prejudice than by the facts of the case. Prejudice may arise in a number of ways and prejudicial evidence generally will not be admitted unless its probative value is very high. An example of prejudicial evidence is the use of a prior criminal record to suggest guilt with respect to a subsequent offence.

HEARSAY

The concept of hearsay can be a confusing one. The technical definition of hearsay is testimony or documentary evidence given in court about a statement made outside court, which is offered to prove the truth of what was said outside court.

However, in commonsense terms, we all understand that hearsay arises when a witness relates secondhand information. This is usually a case of person A testifying to what he or she was told by person B, where person B is unwilling or unavailable to testify. This type of testimony is regarded as weak because the statement does not reflect the firsthand knowledge of the witness, and also because the person who originally made it is not available for cross-examination. Thus the general rule is that all hearsay statements are inadmissible in court.

Hearsay Exceptions

A multitude of exceptions to the general rule excluding hearsay have evolved over time in the courts. Generally, if a piece of hearsay evidence is both necessary and seemingly reliable, there will be an exception that fits that particular case. However, because there are often situations where a piece of evidence is both necessary and reliable, but does not fit a recognized exception, the common law has created a more general rule that hearsay that is both necessary and reliable will be admitted.

Business Records

Business records are documentary hearsay evidence in the sense that the people who actually made the records—employees in various capacities—are not present to testify. Thus the evidence is secondhand. The person who recorded the information is usually not present in court because he or she is unknown, and even if known, he or she would be unlikely to remember having made that exact record, and thus could not testify to having done so. Since the person who introduces the business records to the court is not the person who made the documents, they are secondhand information and are considered hearsay.

Take, for example, the business records of a bank, which include account forms, loan forms, credit information on clients, and so forth. Since many employees have access to the same files, it becomes impossible to determine exactly which employee actually recorded each transaction. Later, a transaction may become important evidence in a criminal investigation, but it would likely be pointless to attempt to ascertain who recorded that a Mr. Edwards withdrew $2000 on Wednesday, February 5, for example.

The reason why these records should be admissible is simply that they are inherently reliable. Banks, manufacturers, retail businesses, and so forth rely on their records being truthful and accurate, and hence should have no reason to exaggerate or hide facts. The assumption is that businesses generally have no motive to fabricate. Naturally, if such a motive is found, the records become inadmissible.

Under s. 30 of the *Canada Evidence Act*, business records are to be admitted in evidence as long as they are made in the "usual and ordinary course of business." The courts have developed a similar rule regarding declarations in the course of duty, which includes both written and oral declarations in a business setting as long as they are (1) made contemporaneously, (2) made in the ordinary course of duty, (3) made by persons having personal knowledge of the matters in question, (4) made by persons who are under a duty to make the record or report, (5) made by persons having no motive to misrepresent the matters. Thus, in court, business records constitute *prima facie* **evidence** of their contents.

prima facie **evidence**
evidence that is reliable on first impression, and that is accepted in the absence of any challenge to its validity

Historical Facts and Materials Relied on by Experts

It would clearly be ridiculous if experts had to account for all the information, theories, and so forth that they rely on in coming to their conclusions, but technically it is all secondhand information. Consider the example of an expert accountant who relies on mathematical theories to reach his conclusions, and who is called on to testify in a trial. To avoid the hearsay prohibition, he would have to fill in the chain of evidence that enabled him to reach his conclusions on the matter before the court, and thus have to call all the mathematicians who originally formulated those theories. The courts have decided that this is impractical, and thus the hearsay foundation for expertise is not treated as problematic (Paciocco, 1996, p. 129).

Spontaneous Statements

Spontaneous statements, sometimes referred to by the Latin term *res gestae*, are statements made in immediate reaction to a particular event. They are thought to be reliable because they do not generally allow time for concoction. For example, if Sally exclaimed, "That guy is going 180 km/h," just as a car was passing by, and was overheard by Edward, Edward would be permitted to testify about what Sally said, because her statement was spontaneous and contemporaneous. Several types of spontaneous statements are covered by this exception to the hearsay rule:

1. *Statements of present physical condition*   These occur when a person claims to be experiencing a particular physical condition. Jim works at a cement factory. He attempts to pick up a heavy bag, drops it suddenly, and grabs his back, exclaiming, "Oh! My back!" His co-worker Patrick overhears him, and hence could repeat Jim's exclamation in court. Patrick's evidence would be admissible, but only to prove that Jim was experiencing the condition at the time, and to establish the duration of the experience (Paciocco, 1996, p. 105).

2. *Statements of present mental state*   These occur when a person describes his or her present state of mind (emotion, intent, motive, plan). For example, if Edweena told George that she was very depressed the night before she was found in a bathtub with her wrists slashed, George would be allowed to repeat that statement in court.

    Naturally, a statement of this kind is admissible only when state of mind is relevant, because (as was discussed earlier) mental state is not always material or relevant. This exception further requires that the person whose state of mind is in question be deceased (Paciocco, 1996, p. 107). So if Edweena had not died, George would not be able to repeat in court what he heard her say. She would be available to testify herself.

    If the statements are explicit statements relating to a state of mind, as in the Edweena example, they are simply admitted as exceptions to the hearsay rule. If a statement permits one to draw an inference about the speaker's state of mind, it is regarded as original testimonial evidence and admitted as circumstantial evidence from which a state of mind can be inferred. So if Edweena had told George that she did not want to go to a party that night, an inference may be drawn from her statement and from evidence that she usually enjoyed parties, that her mental state was not good. Thus, such a statement would be admitted as circumstantial evidence that she may have been depressed.

3. *Excited utterances*   These types of statements relate to a startling event or condition and may be admitted to prove the truth of their contents if they are made while the person making the statement (the declarant) is affected by stress or excitement caused by the event or condition. Assume, for example, that after Rachel's handbag is taken from her in the street, she immediately points at someone and claims, "Hey—he took my handbag!" A passerby, Henry, notices her shouting and pointing. Because she was excited by the immediacy of the event, Henry would be able to relate to the court what Rachel had said. The important criterion is that the statement was made in response to an event, making the possibility of concoction extremely unlikely. For the statement to be sufficiently spontaneous, the link between the declaration and the exciting event must be so close that the mind of the declarant is, in essence, still dominated by the event.

4. *Statements of present sense impressions*   These are statements that describe or explain an event or condition made while a person is experiencing an event or condition, or immediately thereafter. These statements are different from excited utterances because the declarant need not be excited by the actual event. For example, if Tom witnesses a big man pummelling a smaller man during a bar fight and says to Ralph, "Boy, that guy should go pick on someone his own size," Ralph will be able to testify to what Tom said. Such statements are considered reliable since they are made during or just after an incident, leaving little time for fabrication or forgetfulness. Moreover, there is often the added safeguard that the declarant is present in court for cross-examination.

Testimony Given on a Previous Occasion

Statements that people have made to the court on previous occasions may also be admitted for the truth of their contents. For example, if a witness testifies at a **preliminary hearing** (a hearing held to determine whether there is enough evidence to proceed to trial), but then moves to Barbados and is unavailable to testify at trial, his or her testimony will most likely be admitted as evidence of the truth of its contents.

preliminary hearing
a hearing held before the real trial to determine preliminary issues, such as whether there is enough evidence to proceed to trial

The requirements of this hearsay exception are codified in s. 715 of the *Criminal Code*, which provides that a witness's previously recorded evidence may be admitted at trial when any of the following tests are met: (1) the evidence was given at a previous trial on the same charge; (2) the evidence was taken during the investigation of the charge against the accused or at a preliminary inquiry into the charge; (3) the witness refuses to be sworn or to give evidence; or (4) facts are proved on oath from which it can be reasonably inferred that the person is dead, has since become and is insane, is so ill that he or she is unable to travel or testify, or is absent from Canada. Where it is proved that the witness's evidence was taken in the presence of the accused, it may be read as evidence in the proceedings without further proof, unless the accused proves that he or she did not have a full opportunity to cross-examine the witness. In most cases, evidence admitted under this exception is presented by means of **affidavit** (a written document, the truth of which the **affiant** "swears" before a witness).

affidavit
a written and witnessed statement of evidence that the maker swears and signs as proof of its truth

affiant
a person who makes and swears an affidavit

Admissions of a Party

Admissions are acts or words of a party, usually the accused, offered as evidence against that party. Admissions are often lumped in with the hearsay exceptions, even though they really do not possess the same dangers as regular hearsay. The original declarant, being the accused, must be present at his or her own trial, and of course does not need to cross-examine himself or herself.

admissions
acts or words of a party offered as evidence against that party

Admissions of a party also include admissions by conduct, admissions by silence, vicarious admissions (admitting something through an agent, employee, or other third party), and admissions by co-conspirators. For example, fleeing the scene of a crime may be an admission by conduct. This is circumstantial evidence of guilt, based on the idea of **consciousness of guilt**. In other words, the idea is that if one is guilty, one behaves in a certain way. An example of an admission by silence may be the testimony of a friend of the accused who states, "I asked him if he killed her, and he just looked at me and said nothing."

For vicarious and co-conspirator admissions to be admitted as evidence against the accused, they must be adopted by that party as true, either expressly or by implication. Thus the adverse party must adduce evidence to prove that the statement was actually adopted in addition to the hearsay statement. For example, if Bill and Bob plan to rob a convenience store, and Bob is heard by the store owner to say, "Let's just grab the money and go," this statement may also be admissible against Bill as long as one can prove that Bill adopted Bob's view. Thus if there is evidence that Bill nodded or grinned after Bob spoke, that may constitute implied adoption.

Statements Against Interest

Statements against interest are statements made by a declarant that are against his or her best interests, whether property, pecuniary (financial), or penal interests. For example, the statement, "I owe Jonny $6000," is a statement against the declarant's pecuniary interest. The statement, "I haven't kept up with my car payments for months now," is a statement against property interest. The statement, "They never caught me the last time I embezzled from the company," is a statement against penal interest (meaning that if this statement were pursued, penal—punishable—consequences might follow).

These statements are considered reliable because people generally do not make statements that admit facts contrary to their interests unless those statements are true.

Certain conditions must apply for these statements to be admissible. A statement must involve the immediate prejudice of the declarant, meaning that as soon as the declarant makes the statement, he or she must feel the gravity of the consequences of such an admission. The declarant must be unavailable to testify and the witness adducing the evidence must have firsthand knowledge of the statement. Also, this exception essentially applies only to non-parties, meaning that statements against the accused's interests are not covered here but are dealt with in other exceptions.

Prior Inconsistent Statements

Prior inconsistent statements are statements made prior to trial that are inconsistent with the testimony of the witness at trial. For example, if shortly after a crime is committed a witness makes a statement at a police station implicating the accused, but then changes his or her mind and

---

consciousness of guilt
a state of mind that (some believe) is capable of proof and that may support the actual guilt of the person experiencing it

statements against interest
statements made by a person that seem to acknowledge guilt, a debt, etc.—the opposite of self-serving statements

prior inconsistent statements
statements made prior to trial that are inconsistent with statements made at trial

tells the court a completely different story at trial, the original statement made to the police may be admitted for the truth of its contents as long as certain criteria are met. At the very least, it may be admitted to show that the witness is untrustworthy.

This type of statement may be admissible only if it satisfies the important tests of necessity and reliability. A statement is made more reliable if it is taken by the police in very particular circumstances:

1. If the declarant is **under oath** or warned of the possible consequences of **perjury**.

2. If the statement is videotaped.

Also, the statement will be considered more reliable if there is an opportunity to **cross-examine** the declarant.

under oath
(in court) having sworn on the Bible to be truthful

perjury
lying while under oath or affirmation

cross-examination
questioning a witness for the opposing side of the case

Dying Declarations

Dying declarations are statements made by someone who has a hopeless expectation of almost immediate death, and are admissible for the prosecution or the defence. For example, Mindy is repeatedly stabbed in the abdomen by her ex-lover, is found by her mother, and just as she is about to die identifies the killer to her mother. The only stipulations regarding this exception are that the statement must be about the circumstances of the death (meaning it would have been admissible had the deceased been able to testify), and the offence in question must be the homicide of the deceased. Clearly, in these situations such a hearsay exception is necessary. Imagine how ridiculous it would be if the last words of a murder victim were inadmissible. The justice system's belief in the reliability of these statements is based on the idea that a person who knows that he or she is about to die will normally be truthful.

The Principled Approach

Despite the many somewhat confusing exceptions, the trend in hearsay admissibility is to follow the "principled approach." This involves looking at each piece of hearsay evidence on a case-by-case basis. Hearsay evidence will be admitted if it is both *necessary* and *reliable*. That is, if for some legitimate reason the out-of-court speaker is not available to give evidence—and thus the evidence is necessary—and there are good reasons to accept that the out-of-court speaker's statements are reliable, despite the fact that his or her evidence is secondhand and cannot be challenged in court. This avoids some of the more complicated exceptions that have evolved.

The principled approach was adopted after the Supreme Court of Canada decided the *R v. Khan* case in 1990. In that case, a four-year-old girl complained to her mother immediately after leaving the dentist's office that the dentist had put his "birdie" in her mouth. Semen was found on the child's dress, but the child was clearly too young to testify. The

Supreme Court allowed the mother to tell the court what the child had said, despite the fact that this was hearsay evidence and no specific exception applied. The court reached its decision based only on the necessity and reliability of the evidence. The evidence was necessary because it was the foundation of the charge, but the child was not available as a witness. It was also found to be reliable. The court found, based on social-scientific expert testimony, that children usually do not lie about such issues at that age, and also found the statement to be spontaneous. Thus, the court found that the mother's evidence would go toward proving that the child had made the complaint, and support the truth of what the child had said.

Since the *Khan* decision, other decisions regarding admissibility have been decided solely on the necessity and reliability of the hearsay evidence. This appears to be a sort of gap-filler for important hearsay evidence that is not caught by the traditional exceptions.

Weight To Be Given to Hearsay

If hearsay evidence is ruled admissible by the judge, it may still be given less weight than firsthand evidence. Its weight will depend on the quality of the hearsay, but also on the credibility of the witness who relates the hearsay to the court. The jury will usually be told to look to other evidence in the case for corroboration.

SUMMARY

1. The basic rule for hearsay evidence is that a witness cannot repeat in court what he or she heard someone else say.

2. There are many exceptions to the hearsay rule.

3. If a piece of hearsay evidence does not fit a specific exception, it may still be admissible if it is *necessary* and *reliable*.

OPINION EVIDENCE

When a witness expresses his or her opinion on the stand, this is "opinion evidence." The statement, "Billy was always a troubled child," is an opinion, whereas "I have seen Billy howl at the moon on many occasions" is simply a statement of fact as observed by the witness. The general rule is that opinion evidence is not admissible. In our system it is up to the judge or jury—not witnesses—to form opinions. The role of the witness is simply to recount facts that he or she has observed (Paciocco, 1996, p. 113). This is particularly important with regard to ultimate issues (issues central to the case) and oath helping:

1. *Ultimate issue rule/giving opinions on the law*   In the past any opinion that dealt with the very issue at the crux of a case would not be

admissible. It was thought that such opinions would overly influence the court, when the ultimate issue ought to be decided by the judge or jury alone. This rule is no longer considered valid, because it leads to awkward, disjointed, and incomplete testimony. So that the judge or jury can have the most complete picture possible for reaching a conclusion on the ultimate issue, a witness should be allowed to fully describe his or her observations.

Even though witnesses may express thoughts that touch on the ultimate issue, one thing they may *not* do is express their descriptions or opinions in legal terms. For example, a witness may not testify that a driver was "negligent," because negligence has a specific legal meaning. Instead, the witness simply has to describe how the car careened into oncoming traffic (or whatever) and avoid drawing legal conclusions.

2. *Oath helping is generally not permitted* **Oath helping** occurs when a witness expresses an opinion on the credibility of other witnesses. For example, if an expert witness is called to testify that in his or her expert opinion a witness is telling the truth because that type of witness is generally truthful, this evidence will not be admitted, for it is simply evidence that bolsters the idea that the complainant is telling the truth. There is no other merit to that evidence and it does not advance the search for the truth. It is generally believed that this type of evidence may unduly influence the judge or jury without really adding to the fact-finding process (Paciocco, 1996, p. 118).

oath helping
when one witness (improperly) expresses an opinion about the credibility of another witness

The Opinion Rules

Despite the court's reluctance to allow opinion evidence, there are exceptions that permit both lay witnesses and expert witnesses to offer opinions.

Lay witnesses may express their opinions in the following circumstances:

lay witness
any witness testifying about a subject matter in which he or she is not an expert

1. *Where they are uniquely able to provide an opinion* There are certain circumstances where ordinary witnesses (as opposed to expert witnesses) are uniquely able to provide an opinion. An example is the opinion of a witness about the handwriting of a co-worker with whom he or she works closely. Clearly, the witness will be familiar with that person's handwriting and be able to identify it (or not) better than a judge or jury—and perhaps as well as an expert. A similar exception is made for voice recognition (for example, of a voice on a tape recording).

2. *Where the conclusion is one that people of ordinary experience are able to reach* There are certain conclusions that the average witness is considered able to reach without any expertise. For example, the courts have decided that laypeople are generally able to judge when someone is drunk, for drunkenness is a common experience that most people are familiar with. Thus a lay witness will be allowed to

state in court, "I think he was drunk when I saw him." The speed of a car is another example of a subject on which the average layperson will be allowed to give an opinion. A lay witness will be allowed to say, "Well, I was going the limit—so he must have been going at least 150 km/h," or words to that effect.

3. *Where the opinion is part and parcel of the witness's narration*   This third exception to the rule against lay witnesses expressing opinions is the broadest. It recognizes that the distinction between opinion and fact is often artificial, and that witnesses' testimony is usually based largely on opinions or a mixture of facts and opinions. For example, when a witness identifies an accused person in court, he or she is really stating, "This is the person who robbed me … who hijacked the plane … who I saw coming out of the building," or whatever, which is an opinion, not a fact. Clearly, testimony would become disjointed and awkward if all opinions were weeded out. Accordingly, this rule enables a witness to effectively communicate his or her story, including conclusions, uninterrupted by the rule that forbids opinions. Ultimately, it is up to the judge to decide whether he or she will allow these opinions to be admitted into evidence.

Testimony from experts is also essentially opinion evidence. If it is necessary and relevant, if the expert is properly qualified, and if there is no exclusionary rule that would prevent him or her from testifying, the evidence may be admissible. Take, for example, a case involving a fatal shooting, where a bloodspatter expert's testimony may help to recreate the circumstances of the homicide. The prosecution will have to prove that the opinion is both necessary (that is, that non-experts are incapable of interpreting bloodspatter patterns) and relevant (that is, that it advances the search for the truth). Finally, the prosecution will have to prove that the expert has the proper credentials and training.

SUMMARY

The general rule is that witnesses are not allowed to give their opinions on the stand. In particular:

1. Witnesses may not express their observations in legal terms.

2. Evidence that bolsters witness credibility (oath helping) is not permitted.

3. Lay witnesses may give their opinion if

    a. they are uniquely able to provide an opinion,

    b. where the conclusion is one that people of ordinary experience can make, and

    c. the opinion is part of the narrative.

4. Expert opinion evidence is permitted if it is necessary and relevant.

CHARACTER EVIDENCE

Character evidence is any evidence that goes to establishing personality, attitude, general capacity, or the propensity to behave a certain way. As a general rule, character evidence is *not* admissible, but there are many exceptions. Character can be proved in a number of ways, which may also involve particular rules of evidence that must be kept in mind. There are four ways to prove character:

1. circumstantial evidence describing certain acts from which inferences can be drawn,

2. opinion evidence,

3. evidence of reputation in the community, and

4. expert psychiatric evidence.

Exceptions to the General Rule

The exceptions to the general rule are stricter when the prosecution wants to introduce character evidence *against* the accused.

Character Evidence Rules: The Prosecution

1. An exception exists if character is *directly in issue* in the case. For example, if an accused is using the defence of mental disorder, psychiatric testimony is clearly necessary. The dangerous offender provisions of the *Criminal Code*, which require evidence of the convict's character, provide another example.

2. If the accused chooses to put forward evidence of good character or otherwise claims to have a good character, the prosecution is permitted to cross-examine such testimony and is permitted to put specific examples of *bad character* to the witness to weaken the force of the witness's evidence. The prosecution is permitted to do so only when the accused has first initiated the discussion of his or her character (called "putting character in issue"). For example, if the accused's neighbour is asked to testify by the defence and begins to say what a great person the accused is, the prosecution will be able to rebut this by demonstrating that the accused, for example, has a criminal record (thereby alluding to evidence that would otherwise be too prejudicial to put forward). Therefore, the defence must be very careful not to put the accused's character in issue—unless the accused has an absolutely spotless reputation. Evidence that will not put the accused's character in issue includes

   a. A denial of the crime.

   b. An explanation that fleshes out the defence.

c. A description of the accused's background, such as his or her education and employment history (as long as the defence doesn't stray into philanthropic deeds).

Similar Fact Evidence

similar fact evidence
evidence that suggests that the accused has acted in the past in a way that is similar to the acts alleged as part of the offence being tried

Similar fact evidence is evidence that the accused has committed acts in the past that are markedly similar to the acts alleged in the present charge. Sue, for example, is charged with failing to blow into a Breathalyzer after being stopped for drunk driving. Her defence is that she did not understand the instruction. The prosecution learns that she was convicted of refusing to blow twice before. This might be admissible as similar fact evidence, but it is not evidence that Sue has a propensity to drive drunk, or that she is a bad person generally and is therefore more likely to drive drunk. However, it is evidence that she refused to blow in the past, and therefore understood the instructions on the most recent occasion.

Similar fact evidence is a difficult concept. It raises the issue of prejudice, for it often looks more like propensity evidence than like anything else and care must be taken to meet certain narrow conditions for its admission. Traditionally, any evidence showing that the accused had committed acts similar to those in the charge was admitted as long as the acts were "strikingly similar"—that is, displayed a similar *modus operandi* or "hallmark." An example was the famous "brides in the bath" case, which concerned a husband who had a habit of killing his wives. After the murder of wife number three, who was drowned while taking a bath, the prosecution was allowed to bring forward evidence that wives one and two had died in exactly the same fashion.

Currently, the courts insist that before any similar fact evidence is admitted, there must be a balancing of probative value and prejudice. First, the Crown must show that the evidence is relevant, in the context of a line of reasoning that does not require the judge or jury to infer that the character of the accused is such that he or she is the kind of person to commit the offence, for that would be considered propensity evidence and would be impermissible reasoning (Paciocco, 1996, p. 40).

Assume, for example, that Julie stands accused of brutally and repeatedly stabbing a stranger. The Crown wishes to adduce evidence that Julie has spent time in a mental institution and suffers from schizophrenia, and thus is more likely to have been the perpetrator of this type of frenzied murder. Clearly, the logical inference identifying Julie as the killer is weak. More than anything else, it proposes that Julie is guilty because she is mentally ill, and thus more likely than the average person to have killed someone. This is propensity evidence, and would not be admitted.

Here is an example that might pass this test: Julie stands charged of murdering a stranger, dragging his body into a churchyard, and sewing a cross into the victim's skin. The Crown wishes to adduce evidence that Julie has killed small animals and sewn crosses onto their corpses, and in the past has been charged with cruelty to animals. This presents a situation of strikingly similar facts. The Crown is attempting to infer the identity of the murderer from the similar hallmark of crosses stitched into flesh. Because the Crown is not attempting to say that anyone who does something as bizarre as that is more likely to be a murderer, the evidence will most likely be admitted. In effect, the pattern is a form of identification evidence.

After the Crown proves that it is not using an impermissible type of reasoning, the judge may still exclude the evidence where its probative value does not outweigh the risk of prejudice that it presents. Consider this example: Luke is charged with sexually assaulting a woman. The Crown wishes to adduce evidence that he was previously convicted of sexually assaulting a man. The Crown reasons that this evidence demonstrates that he is unable to control his sexual urges. However, if this scenario passes the first test of impermissible reasoning, it surely fails the second test. The link is not "strikingly similar," for different sexes are involved, and if no better link is established, the prejudice of admitting this evidence will outweigh its probative value. Information such as this is extremely prejudicial, for human nature is such that people cannot help but assume that if someone has raped in the past, he or she will likely do so again. Such evidence must be kept from the jury so that it is able to decide, in an unbiased manner, based on evidence specifically related to the case, whether the accused has been proved guilty.

Character Evidence Rules: The Defence

1. *Good character* evidence about the accused is generally admissible in criminal trials. This flows from the premise that the accused is innocent until proven guilty, and therefore is permitted to rebut the charges brought against him or her by adducing evidence of his or her good character. This exception is limited to evidence of reputation, excluding specific acts of goodness. Thus statements from neighbours, co-workers, and family members that, for example, the accused "is really well-liked by all," are permitted. On the other hand, statements that, for example, the accused "donates $5000 a year to the Humane Society," are not permitted. But remember, this evidence can be rebutted by evidence of "bad" character, because now the accused has put his or her character in issue.

2. *Expert evidence of character* is generally not admissible unless the crime could only have been committed by a member of a group with distinctive psychological characteristics. For example, if a murder was clearly committed by a pedophile, and the accused does not have any of the characteristics of that paraphilia (sexual disorder), expert evidence of the accused's sexual character may be permitted. Recently there has been a trend toward not admitting expert evidence of character, because scientific opinion on certain issues is still in flux, and the evidence may be too heavily weighted, without sufficient scientific grounding.

3. As discussed in chapter 2, *prior convictions* are clearly a good way of sullying the character of witnesses or the accused, and can be extremely prejudicial. The rule regarding the admissibility of prior convictions is different depending on whether it relates to the accused or another witness. Where a person other than the accused is the witness, s. 12 of the *Canada Evidence Act* states that any witness may be cross-examined on his or her criminal record. This rule is subject to the discretion of the judge, who has the right to control this practice and exclude prejudicial evidence. Where the accused is the witness, s. 666 of the *Criminal Code* provides that the accused may be cross-examined on his or her criminal record only after the accused has adduced evidence of his or her good character. In addition, the court always has the discretion to exclude evidence of a prior criminal record if that evidence has little or no probative value (*R v. Corbett*).

4. The defence is also permitted to call evidence to show that someone else is more likely than the accused to have committed the crime. To support a defence such as self-defence, evidence of violence or threats is also admissible.

5. Sections 276 and 277 of the *Criminal Code* provide an important limit on evidence about the character of complainants in sexual abuse cases, by prohibiting evidence about a complainant's other sexual experiences, except in very rare circumstances.

SUMMARY

1. Character evidence is admissible if character is directly in issue.

2. Evidence of the accused's good character is admissible in criminal trials.

3. If the defence brings forward evidence of the accused's good character, the prosecution may introduce evidence to rebut this— that is, evidence of his or her bad character.

4. Expert evidence of character is admissible only if the crime could only have been committed by a member of a group with distinctive psychological characteristics.

5. If similar fact evidence is "strikingly similar," and its probative value outweighs its prejudicial effect, it may be admitted.

6. Sections 276 and 277 of the *Criminal Code* limit the use of evidence about the sexual history of complainants in sexual abuse cases.

privilege
a kind of protection (exemption from admissibility) that attaches to evidence produced in special circumstances, such as in the course of certain classes of relationships

PRIVILEGE

Evidence may be deemed inadmissible if it fits into one of the recognized categories of privilege. **Privilege** is based on the idea that the confidentiality of certain relationships must be respected for society to benefit from their existence. These include the lawyer–client relationship (usually referred to as the solicitor–client relationship), the spousal relationship, and the police–informant relationship. Privilege may in fact work against the truth-seeking role of evidence, for it allows secrets to be kept from the courts. However, since these relationships are considered to benefit society *because* they are not forced to be revealed, they are protected from the normal rules of the court, which place an absolute value on the truth.

For a communication to receive the benefits of privilege, the following tests must be met:

1. The communication must have occurred on the understanding that it would not be disclosed.

2. The confidentiality of the communication must be necessary to maintaining the relationship.

3. The relationship must be one that the courts and the community wish to protect.

4. The injury to the relationship as a result of the disclosure must be greater than the benefit to society of the correct disposal of litigation.

SUMMARY

1. Privilege is based on the idea that the confidentiality of certain relationships must be respected for those relationships to function effectively.

2. Privileged communications do not have to be divulged in court.

IMPROPERLY OBTAINED EVIDENCE

The issue of improperly obtained evidence is particularly important to the police. Generally, the police are responsible for gathering the evidence that proves the Crown's case, and therefore the burden of properly doing that job falls on them. The penalty for not doing it properly is particularly severe: any evidence that is improperly obtained may be excluded under s. 24(2) of the *Canadian Charter of Rights and Freedoms*. This means that if evidence, even against the most heinous of murderers, is gathered improperly—resulting in a Charter violation—it may be excluded and the murderer may be acquitted. This principle can be extremely frustrating, but as long as proper procedures are followed the relevant evidence will be admitted and the police's hard work will pay off.

Improperly obtaining evidence violates the rights guaranteed by the Charter, for example the s. 8 right—highly regarded by everyone—to be free from unreasonable search and seizure. Consider a case where police officers make an unauthorized entry into a private dwelling—that is, they break in without a search warrant—and find a large amount of crack cocaine. That cocaine might be part of a big trafficking operation, but the evidence will not be admitted, for a break-in without lawful authority is an unreasonable search.

The rights guaranteed by the Charter are like trump cards. When a Charter right is violated, the violation overshadows other factors in a case. Charter rights are fundamental individual rights in a democracy, and underpin all other principles in the Canadian criminal justice system. They include:

◆   The right to life, liberty, and security of the person (s. 7).

◆   The right to be secure against unreasonable search or seizure (s. 8).

◆   The right not to be arbitrarily detained or imprisoned (s. 9).

◆   The right on arrest or detention to be informed promptly of the reasons therefor, to retain and instruct counsel without delay and to be informed of that right (s. 10).

◆   Various rights pertaining to proceedings in criminal and penal matters, such as the right to an impartial court (s. 11).

◆   The right not to be subjected to any cruel and unusual treatment or punishment (s. 12).

◆   The right against self-incrimination (s. 13).

However, not every violation of a Charter right will cause evidence to be excluded, for the violation must be a serious one that brings the administration of justice into disrepute.

SUMMARY

1. Evidence is considered illegally obtained if it violates the accused's rights under the *Charter of Rights and Freedoms*.

2. Illegally obtained evidence may be excluded from the trial if certain conditions are met.

KEY TERMS

admissibility	prior inconsistent statements
weight	under oath
prima facie evidence	perjury
preliminary hearing	cross-examination
affidavit	oath helping
affiant	lay witness
admissions	similar fact evidence
consciousness of guilt	privilege
statements against interest	

REVIEW

■ TRUE OR FALSE?

_____ 1. When evidence is less reliable it is given less weight.

_____ 2. If a witness said on the stand that "Bobby gave me the car," this would be hearsay.

_____ 3. Business records are considered hearsay, but they are admitted anyway.

_____ 4. Hearsay evidence will not be admitted if it does not fit one of the recognized exceptions.

_____ 5. The "principled approach" refers to a school of thought that prohibits all hearsay from being admitted.

_____ 6. The statement, "I think he was drunk," is opinion evidence and would not be admissible.

_____ 7. In the past, witnesses could not comment on the "ultimate issue" in the trial. This is no longer the case.

_____ 8. "Oath helping" refers to situations where counsel attempt to bolster the credibility of their witnesses.

_____ 9. Bad character evidence is always admissible against the accused, because convictions would be impossible without it.

_____ 10. Privileged information need not be revealed in court.

■ MULTIPLE CHOICE

1. Hearsay evidence is considered unreliable because

   a. people will say anything to get out of a tight spot

   b. the witness may be prone to misstate what he has heard another person say

   c. it amounts to oath helping

   d. there is no way of telling whether the person whose words are allegedly being repeated actually made the statement

2. The term "statements against interest" refers to

   a. confession evidence

   b. statements given by the opposing party

   c. statements that are against the declarant's property, pecuniary, or penal interests

   d. an exception to the hearsay rule

   e. c and d

3. Opinion evidence may be admissible when

    a. the opinion is inextricably linked to the narrative

    b. experts give their testimony

    c. the opinion is one that the witness is uniquely able to give

    d. all of the above

4. If the Crown is permitted by the judge to introduce detailed information about the accused's prior convictions, the judge has probably based his or her decision on

    a. the issues of necessity and reliability

    b. the presence of facts strikingly similar to those of the case at hand

    c. the fact that the Crown requested a special dispensation

    d. the fact that evidence of the accused's good character was introduced by the defence

5. When evidence is improperly obtained

    a. a mistrial is declared and everyone has to start all over again

    b. it may be excluded from the trial

    c. the police are disciplined

    d. the accused's rights are infringed

    e. b and d

■ SHORT ANSWER

1. "As I came in I saw Jim lying on the carpet in a pool of blood. He tried to raise his head and blurted out, 'Someone broke in—some big bearded guy—we struggled and he shot me.' Then the ambulance took Jim to the hospital and he died that night." Would this statement be admissible? Why?

2. A key witness for the prosecution moved to Cyprus and the police have lost contact with her. She testified at the preliminary hearing, though. What can the Crown do?

3. If children are too young to testify, but make an immediate complaint to a parent, are there circumstances in which their parents can, in essence, testify for them? What are these circumstances?

4. A witness stated, "I know what I saw. It was a clear case of reckless and impaired driving." Would counsel object to such a statement? If so, why?

5. Define "oath helping."

CHAPTER 4

The Bloody Glove: Physical and Documentary Evidence

CHAPTER OBJECTIVES

After completing this chapter, you should be able to:

◆ Differentiate between real, demonstrative, and view evidence.

◆ Discuss the problems associated with videotape and photographic evidence.

◆ Explain the "best evidence rule."

PHYSICAL EVIDENCE

Types of Physical Evidence

Physical evidence is evidence that takes the form of actual objects, as opposed to testimony. There are several types of physical evidence:

1. *Real evidence*   **Real evidence** includes objects directly linked to the occurrence or crime—that is, objects that "speak" for themselves—such as the gun used in a murder or the counterfeit bills used in a counterfeiting scheme. Real evidence is relevant only if it is authentic. The introduction into evidence of a bloody shirt that connects the accused to a murder will have relevance only if it is the same shirt taken from the murder scene. Therefore, there is a need to preserve the integrity of the object. As discussed in chapter 2, the party introducing the object must be able to show that it has not been tampered with or otherwise contaminated. This is how the Crown establishes continuity.

real evidence
physical objects (including documents in some cases) with a direct link to the crime that are introduced as evidence

2. *Demonstrative evidence*   **Demonstrative evidence** encompasses items that help to explain or illustrate the testimony of a witness—that is, evidence that demonstrates something. Demonstrative evidence includes items such as photographs, videotapes, maps, charts, and anatomically correct dolls. Different standards of admissibility apply depending on the type of demonstrative evidence:

demonstrative evidence
evidentiary "tools" produced by a party to help explain a case, such as maps or photographs of the crime scene

---

51

a. *Photographs and videotapes* The admissibility of photographs and videotapes of the crime itself, of the crime scene, or of the crime's aftermath depends on several factors (Paciocco, 1996, p. 240):

   i. Accuracy in representing the facts.

   ii. Fairness and absence of any intention to mislead.

   iii. Verification on oath by a person capable of doing so.

The person verifying authenticity does not need to be the cameraman. An eyewitness, for example, can also confirm that the photo or video is a fair and accurate reproduction of the scene as it looked at the time of the incident.

The problem with this type of evidence is that it tends to be very powerful and may have a sensational effect on the judge or jury. A picture is worth a thousand words, but photos and videos can present a distorted version of reality: the angle of a shot, the lighting, and special effects such as slow motion can create a more sinister impression than is justified and thereby prejudice the accused's case and mislead the court. The issue is not how grotesque or shocking a photo or video is, but its probative value—how accurate it is in portraying what actually happened. That is why photographic and videotape evidence *must* be associated with testimonial evidence if the judge and jury are to draw conclusions from it.

Consider a case where two men agree to fight and one man is killed, although the surviving combatant did not intend to kill. The death goes unreported and the body begins to decay. Three weeks later the body is discovered and the police photograph the crime scene and the body. Should the photos of the decayed victim be admissible in the ensuing homicide trial? Probably not, for they may prejudice the accused's case and mislead the court. Although it was the accused's fault that the victim died, photos of a decayed victim do not accurately convey anything about how the homicide occurred, but could inordinately disgust the judge or jury.

b. *Maps, charts, and visual aids* These can help witnesses explain, and judges and juries understand, concepts and theories referred to in testimony. They can also make it easier to visualize locations. For example, in a case where several accomplices used cellular phones to communicate with one another, and their calls were traced through nearby transmission towers, a witness might find a map of those towers very helpful for describing the locations of the co-conspirators. Another example of the use of visual aids is an expert's use of a chart or diagram to explain blood typing or DNA matching.

The only questions that must be answered before visual aids are admitted into the courtroom are as follows:

    i.   Does the visual aid help the witness explain his or her testimony to the judge and jury?

    ii.   Does it help the judge and jury understand the witness's testimony?

If these criteria are satisfied the aid will be admissible.

3.   *Views or "look-sees"*   **"Having a view"** or a **"look-see"** occurs when the entire court visits the crime scene. Because they are costly and time consuming, and the court's time is precious, look-sees are rare. Only when pictures or a re-creation simply do not do justice to the physical reality of a crime scene, or the parties cannot agree on what constitutes an accurate representation of the scene, may a look-see be permitted. For example, if, in a reckless driving case, an oddity of the street corner in question is best perceived in person, a view may be allowed.

    The rule on what a court is permitted to conclude from a view is set out in an older English case: "Where the matter for decision is one of ordinary common sense, the judge of fact is entitled to form his own judgement on the real evidence of a view, just as much as on the oral evidence of witnesses" (Lord Denning in *Buckingham v. Daily News Ltd.*).

"having a view/look-see"
an excursion by the judge and/ or jury to a site outside the courtroom to view evidence that cannot reasonably be presented in court

Introduction of Exhibits in Court

The trial judge rules on the admissibility of **exhibits**, whether real or documentary evidence. The threshold of proof is not high: the judge must simply be satisfied that there is evidence to support the conclusion that the exhibit is what the party claims it is.

    Once it is ruled admissible, the item is incorporated into the record. This means that the court clerk gives the item an exhibit number, and the court clerk and court reporter record the number and note what the exhibit consists of. Once the exhibit is admitted, the trier of fact makes the final determination of its authenticity, and determines what weight to attach to the evidence.

exhibit
any piece of evidence (real, demonstrative, or documentary) other than oral testimony that is "entered" in the trial record

Continuity: Evidence Free of Taint

The Crown must establish the **continuity** of the exhibit, so that the exhibit is accounted for from the moment it was collected at the scene until it is presented in court. The police officer who found the item at the scene, the detective who then took possession of it, and the identification officer who ultimately assumed its care and custody will all have to be called. The calling of these witnesses may be dispensed with where opposing counsel concede the authenticity or continuity of the evidence. Frequently, in the interest of conserving court time, opposing counsel may well concede continuity unless there are real questions about it. However, one cannot count on a concession, and for this reason preserving the

continuity
in the context of physical evidence, an ability to account for the whereabouts of the evidence (and the identity of those who have had access to it) from the time of its collection to the time it is entered as an exhibit in the trial record

chain of continuity is an important part of gathering and preserving evidence.

SUMMARY

1. Real evidence means objects directly related to the crime—objects that "speak" for themselves.

2. Demonstrative evidence helps to illustrate or explain testimony.

3. Views or look-sees are the rare occasions when the entire court goes to a location that is at issue in the trial.

4. Ensuring the continuity of a piece of physical evidence is key to its admissibility.

DOCUMENTARY EVIDENCE

Best Evidence Rule

best evidence rule
a legal rule requiring that wherever possible, the original document (the best evidence), rather than a reproduction, should be introduced in evidence

The **best evidence rule** requires, whenever possible, that any document of importance to the case be introduced into evidence in its original form. Oral description of the document, or reference to the document in a different document, will generally not suffice. Even photocopies or facsimiles of a document may not satisfy the best evidence rule, because it is possible to produce a document that has been altered in a way that can be almost impossible to detect.

Criminal charges are so serious that the courts have always wanted the best evidence they can get. Over time the courts concluded that they should consider only original evidence whenever possible, because originals are the most accurate source of the information they contained. An example of this meticulous tradition is the rule prohibiting hearsay testimony, which is based on the idea that the best evidence is that provided by the person who actually made the statement.

It is often defence counsel who argue that the court should be presented with the original evidence; however, the rule applies equally to the prosecution and the defence.

Secondary Documentary Evidence

secondary documentary evidence
a piece of documentary evidence that is other than an original, such as a photocopy

If a party can satisfy the court that the original document is lost, destroyed, or otherwise unobtainable, the best evidence rule may be relaxed to allow the introduction of copies or **secondary documentary evidence**. Some recognized exceptions include

1. Instances where someone other than the accused has the original. In this case the prosecutor will serve the third party with a subpoena. If the person refuses to comply or is outside the jurisdiction, secondary evidence may be admitted.

2. Instances where the original cannot be found after due search.

3. Instances where production of the original is impossible, as in the case of an inscription on a tombstone.

4. Instances where statutory provisions allow the introduction of certified copies of government, banking, or business records. Sections 25-30 of the *Canada Evidence Act* contain such provisions. Section 29, for example, provides that "a copy of any entry in any book or record kept in any financial institution shall in all legal proceedings be admitted in evidence as proof."

5. Instances where the original has been destroyed.

Generally, flexibility is used when applying the best evidence rule, for an overzealous application of the rule succeeds only in hampering the search for the truth.

Authenticating Documentary Evidence

For documents to be tendered as proof of their contents—that is, as direct, not secondary, evidence—they must be shown to be authentic. There are several ways of proving that documents are authentic and thereby introducing them into evidence:

1. The maker of the document can be called to testify that the document is indeed what he or she wrote, and that it represents a true statement of fact.

2. A witness who saw the document signed or who is familiar with the document can be called to testify.

3. Where handwriting is an issue:

    a. A witness who is familiar with the handwriting in question (for example, of a co-worker or family member) can be called to testify.

    b. The writing in dispute can be compared with writing that the court has already determined is genuine.

    c. Experts who specialize in identifying handwriting can be called to testify.

4. The opposing party can concede that the document is authentic.

5. If a document written by another person is used in the cross-examination of an accused and the accused accepts it as true, the contents of the document become evidence. But if he or she refuses to accept the document as true, its contents cannot be accepted as evidence against him or her. Nevertheless, if the accused has in some way recognized, adopted, or acted on the contents of the document—without having expressly accepted it—the document may be used against the accused.

6. When a document is shown to a witness to refresh his memory and though the witness has no present recollection (does not remember the writing) after seeing it, he accepts its validity as past recollection recorded (a record of what he or she remembered at one time), the document can be admitted as direct evidence.

7. According to s. 30 of the *Canada Evidence Act*, documents made in the ordinary course of business are admissible without the need for testimonial evidence.

8. Documents found in the accused's possession are generally admissible against the accused. However, they must be shown to be relevant to the issues in the trial.

SUMMARY

1. The best evidence rule means that the original document should be used as evidence whenever possible.

2. Secondary evidence may be acceptable if the original is proved to be lost, stolen, or otherwise irretrievable.

3. For documents to be admissible they must be found to be authentic.

KEY TERMS

real evidence   continuity

demonstrative evidence   best evidence rule

"having a view/look-see"   secondary documentary evidence

exhibit

REVIEW

■ TRUE OR FALSE?

_____ 1. Documentary evidence includes the testimony of witnesses.

_____ 2. A bloody lampshade would be considered real evidence.

_____ 3. A video of a crime scene is called a view.

_____ 4. A photocopy is acceptable under the best evidence rule.

_____ 5. Only an expert can use handwriting to determine an author's identity.

■ MULTIPLE CHOICE

1. Demonstrative evidence can include

   a. maps and charts

   b. anatomical models

   c. videotapes and photographs

   d. all of the above

2. Continuity always needs to be proved, unless

   a. the documents are lost or stolen

   b. the opposing party concedes that the exhibit is authentic

   c. the officers are not available to testify

   d. the supervisory officer testifies on behalf of all the officers involved

3. The best evidence rule is important because

   a. the defence often uses stalling tactics to delay the trial, and making the Crown produce originals can be a tedious and lengthy process

   b. criminal charges are very serious

   c. it has evolved over time and is necessary for upholding the common law tradition

   d. quality, not quantity, is what is important

■ SHORT ANSWER

1. Why might a videotape showing the accused grimacing with rage be found inadmissible?

2. Explain why business documents are normally admitted into evidence without the need for testimony. Which section of the *Canada Evidence Act* allows this?

3. What questions must be answered before demonstrative evidence is permitted?

■ FILL IN THE BLANKS

1. A chart depicting DNA typing is _____ evidence.

2. The _____ provides that original documents should be used whenever possible.

3. The court _____ gives exhibits a number when they are admitted into evidence.

4. When a piece of evidence is proved to be free of taint, the requirement of _____ has been satisfied.

5. Moving the entire court to another location is called a

    _____.

CHAPTER 5
Oral Evidence and Witnesses

CHAPTER OBJECTIVES

After completing this chapter, you should be able to:

◆ Explain the meaning of competence and compellability.

◆ Name and define the different categories of privilege.

◆ Describe when expert evidence will be admissible.

◆ Explain the significance of prior statements.

◆ Describe the procedure for admitting prior inconsistent statements.

◆ Describe the order and style of questioning of witnesses.

Witnesses are called by the Crown or the defence to give evidence that will prove the story of the side that calls them. Almost anyone can be a witness: the accused, the victim (if there is one), members of the public (often called lay witnesses), police officers, and experts. There are rules, however, governing who can testify, what they can testify about, and when they can testify. At the most basic level, witnesses must be both competent and compellable.

COMPETENCE

For a potential witness to give evidence, he or she must be **competent** to testify. To be competent means that the witness is legally permitted to testify, which in turn means that the witness has four basic capacities:

competence
being legally permitted to testify (based on the absence of factors such as age under 14 years or mental handicap)

1. The capacity of perception (the ability to observe and interpret the event in question).

2. The capacity to remember.

3. The capacity for communication (the ability to tell the court what he or she saw, heard, or did).

4. The capacity for sincerity (the understanding that he or she has an obligation to tell the truth and that legal consequences may result from lying on the stand).

Competence is usually an issue only for children and people with mental disorders. Section 16 of the *Canada Evidence Act* prescribes that where witnesses are children under the age of 14 or people whose mental capacity is challenged, the court must conduct an inquiry into the witnesses' competence to testify. This means that the court must determine whether:

oath

a promise to tell the truth that is "sworn" with a hand on the Bible

solemn affirmation

a promise to tell the truth without a hand on the Bible—for the non-religious—as provided for in s. 14 of the Canada Evidence Act

1. They understand the nature of the **oath** or **solemn affirmation** required of them. The oath involves swearing on the Bible; the affirmation simply requires the witness to solemnly agree that he or she will "speak the truth, the whole truth and nothing but the truth" (s. 14 of the *Canada Evidence Act*).

2. They are able to communicate their evidence.

Generally speaking, competence is a fairly easy test to pass. Mental disorder in and of itself will not disqualify a witness from testifying. Even a disposition to lie does not disqualify a witness. Although it may affect the credibility of the witness, it does not affect the assessment of competence.

With regard to the issue of children's competence, there are three possible outcomes from this analysis:

1. When a child understands the oath or affirmation and is able to communicate, he or she is able to testify normally and is treated the same as a competent adult. Here, the child must understand that the oath or affirmation involves a moral obligation to tell the truth in court and that this is over and above ordinary duty in normal social context.

unsworn testimony

testimony given without having sworn an oath or made a solemn affirmation

2. When a child does not understand the oath or affirmation but is able to communicate, he or she will still be able to testify as long as he or she can "promise to tell the truth." This amounts to **unsworn testimony**. In this context, able to communicate means having the capacity to observe, recollect, and communicate verbally. The issue is not whether the evidence is correct, but whether the child has the ability to communicate.

3. When a child does not understand the oath or affirmation and cannot communicate, the child obviously cannot testify.

Unfortunately, young children are most often asked to be witnesses in cases involving abuse, and the accused is often a parent or some other adult who is close to them. This can be very traumatic for children, which is why privacy screens and closed-circuit televisions have been permitted in some instances. Sometimes a videotape of an interview is permitted. If a videotape of a child witness is made, it is very important that the child not be led or influenced by the interviewer, because there is generally no opportunity for cross-examination.

Spouses of accused persons constitute the final category of people who may be deemed incompetent to testify. Under s. 4 of the *Canada Evidence Act*, spouses (legally married husbands and wives of accused persons) are *not* competent witnesses for the prosecution. The marriage relationship is considered important enough that spouses should not be forced to testify against each other. This means that even a husband or wife who wishes to testify against a spouse may not do so. However, if called on by the defence, a husband or wife may testify for the defence. Certain offences involving violence to children or violence between spouses are expressly excluded from this rule. For example, if a man is charged with sexually assaulting a child, his wife will be a competent witness for the prosecution.

After determining whether someone is competent to testify, it must next be determined whether he or she is also compellable.

COMPELLABILITY

To be able to testify, a witness must be **compellable**, meaning that he or she can be legally forced to testify—in other words, subpoenaed. A **subpoena** is a written notice, usually hand-delivered, summoning a named person to court on a certain day, and stating that if the person refuses, penal consequences may follow. In criminal cases nearly everyone is a compellable witness. Again, however, there are exceptions to this rule:

compellability
being without legal excuse (such as status as the accused's spouse) for not testifying

subpoena
a formal request, enforceable by the court, for a person's attendance in court to give testimony

1. A person cannot be compelled to testify against his or her spouse, expect in certain cases of child abuse.

2. Pursuant to s. 11(c) of the *Canadian Charter of Rights and Freedoms*, the accused is *not* compellable:

    11(c) Any person charged with an offence has the right not to be compelled to be a witness in proceedings against that person in respect of the offence.

3. An exception also applies to co-accused who are charged on the same information. Co-accused charged on the same information are "joined" as parties and accordingly are tried together. Thus, it would be unfair to compel one to testify against another, for that would be forcing the co-accused to incriminate themselves and violate s. 11(c) of the Charter. If, however, they are tried separately and charged on separate informations, they may be compelled to testify against one another.

SUMMARY

1. For a witness to testify, he or she must be both competent and compellable.

2. Competence means that a witness is legally permitted to testify. Children, mentally ill people, and spouses may be incompetent in certain circumstances.

3. Compellability means that a witness can be legally forced to testify. Spouses, accused, and co-accused may not be compellable in certain circumstances.

PRIVILEGE

The concept of privilege, which was briefly discussed in chapter 3, is designed to protect certain relationships or privacy interests. The community believes that these relationships should be fostered and that their secrecy should be respected for them to function properly. In addition to the recognized categories of privilege mentioned below, there are some situations in which the courts have approved legal protection against the disclosure of information. Any communication for which privilege is claimed must satisfy the following tests:

1. The communication was made in confidence.

2. This confidence is necessary for maintaining the relationship.

3. The courts and the community wish to protect the relationship.

4. The injury that disclosure would cause is greater than the benefit to society of exposing the information in the communication.

Solicitor–Client Privilege

solicitor–client privilege
an exemption from disclosure requirements for certain communications between a lawyer and client

Solicitor–client privilege protects oral and written communications between lawyer and client. This means that these communications, or knowledge the lawyer has about the client, cannot be disclosed either to the opposing party (which is usually the prosecutor) or to the court. To be considered privileged, and therefore protected, the communications must have been made confidentially and for the purpose of obtaining legal advice or preparing for trial. The privilege is a right of the client (not the lawyer) and may be waived only by the client. The privilege also encompasses any third parties who have had access to the communications for the purpose of providing legal services to the client (for example, secretaries, clerks, and experts).

There is no privilege for communications that

1. Are in furtherance of a criminal offence.

2. Contain information that is necessary for the accused to make full answer and defence.

3. Have been overheard by another party.

4. Are evidenced in documents that have been lost or stolen—that is, that cannot be produced.

The Paul Bernardo murder case is an example of the problems associated with solicitor–client privilege. Bernardo's lawyer, Ken Murray, claims that although he (Murray) knew about certain videotapes the police were looking for (videotapes depicting offences being committed), solicitor–client privilege prevented him from disclosing their existence. Another issue of privilege arises because the Crown wants to force Bernardo's other lawyers to reveal the instructions Bernardo gave them, but

Bernardo refuses to waive his privilege. The Crown is arguing that the Court should order disclosure of the evidence.

Spousal Privilege

As discussed above, spouses do not need to testify against one another in most circumstances. **Spousal privilege** is founded on the idea of maintaining marital harmony and protecting the legal construct of marriage. As stated in s. 4 of the *Canada Evidence Act*, the privilege does not apply to common law, same-sex, irreconcilably separated, or divorced spouses.

> **spousal privilege**
> *an exemption from disclosure and compellability for the spouse of an accused*

The circumstances under which spouses may be compelled to testify are set out in ss. 4(2), 4(3), and 4(5) of the *Canada Evidence Act*, and are as follows:

1. The offence involves one spouse against the other spouse, and affects the person, health, or liberty of the victim spouse.

2. The offence involves an indecent act.

3. The offence involves abduction of children.

4. The offence involves criminal neglect of family members.

5. The offence involves either of the spouses committing theft against the other while living apart or in preparation for desertion.

6. The offence involves an assault against a child under age 14.

There is clearly a need for spouses to be compellable and competent witnesses against each other under these circumstances. Otherwise, wife batterers and child abusers would be able to take advantage of the spousal privilege, knowing that the person most knowledgeable about the crime would be unable to testify.

Public Interest and Unity Privilege

The **public interest and unity privilege** is based on the idea that in certain instances government documents should remain secret for the protection of the public. For example, this privilege has often been granted in situations involving security issues. The state may also claim the privilege on the grounds that to do so will ensure the highest degree of honesty among its operatives, for if the operatives believe that they may be called on at any time to disclose the nature of their work, they will be in the position of having to resort to lies to preserve the integrity and secrecy of their projects. This is not, however, to give credence to the idea that the state is involved in coverups and conspiracies. Consider the example of an undercover police officer gathering evidence against a biker gang. If the officer were forced to reveal his or her undercover identity in court, the operation would be jeopardized, as would the officer's safety and the public's interest in catching violent criminals. Claiming the public interest and unity privilege does not automatically ensure secrecy, for

> **public interest and unity privilege**
> *a class of privilege protecting information the disclosure of which would threaten the public interest, such as, in some cases, the identity of undercover investigators*

it is still up to the judge to exercise discretion, and he or she may choose to review the evidence and disclose all or part of it.

Police Informant Privilege

police informant privilege

a privilege that attaches, in some situations, to the identity of a police informer, such as the provider of a "Crime Stoppers" tip

The police often rely on confidential informants, such as those who contact the police through Crime Stoppers, to give them information about offences. Without a privilege that extends to keeping the identity of the informants secret in court—the **police informant privilege**—people would be loath to report friends and acquaintances for fear of reprisals. Consider the example of a drug dealer's sister. She believes that her brother is out of control and wants to report him to the police, but is afraid that he will react violently if he learns that she reported him. Clearly, confidentiality for this informant is key.

Although the privilege is asserted by the Crown, it exists to protect the informant. There are three situations in which the privilege may be lost and the accused may cross-examine the police regarding an informant's identity:

1. Where the informant is a material witness to the crime. Material witnesses cannot hide behind informant privilege and avoid having to testify, for they have crucial information concerning the crime.

agent provocateur

an informer or agent of the police who seeks to provoke a suspect into committing a crime

2. Where the informant is an **agent provocateur** for the police. An agent provocateur is one who is used by the police to entice people into committing crimes. For example, if the police ask a person off the street to approach a suspected drug dealer and inquire about buying a gram of cocaine (a situation of entrapment, where one is ensnaring a suspect into incriminating himself or herself), that person is an agent provocateur and does not receive the informant privilege.

3. Where the defence suggests that a search was authorized without sufficiently reliable grounds. The information that informants provide is often used by the police to obtain search warrants. Consider the example of Joey, an informant never before used by the police, who tells them that Ivan is a marijuana dealer and gives them Ivan's address. Joey does not tell the police that his girlfriend just dumped him for Ivan, who in fact is not a drug dealer but likes the odd toke. The police obtain a search warrant from a justice of the peace. They search Ivan's address and find only two grams of marijuana, but still charge him with trafficking. Clearly, this is a case where the police have searched a dwelling without sufficient grounds, and the name of the informant is no longer privileged. Another reason why Joey's identity must be divulged is that it helps to prove Ivan's innocence on the trafficking charge.

All of these exceptions flow from the idea that if the informant's identity is necessary to show that the accused is innocent, it must be revealed. This is often called the "innocence at stake" exception.

When police officers are testifying and the issue of informant privilege arises, the phrase commonly used to keep the informant's identity concealed is, "It would not be in the public's interest for me to disclose my source of information."

Privilege Against Self-Incrimination

As was discussed earlier, both the Charter and the *Canada Evidence Act* protect the individual's right not to incriminate himself or herself. The **privilege against self-incrimination** means that a person cannot be incriminated by statements made in past criminal matters and cannot be compelled to testify as a witness against himself or herself. In addition, s. 13 of the Charter provides that an accused who does testify has the right not to have incriminating statements used against him or her in subsequent proceedings.

privilege against self-incrimination
a privilege exempting the accused from the obligation to give self-incriminating evidence (or any evidence at all)

SUMMARY

1. Generally, communications between lawyers and their clients do not have to be divulged to the court.

2. The spousal privilege means that marital partners are not compellable witnesses against one another, except where certain offences are involved.

3. In certain circumstances the state is protected from having to reveal information to the court.

4. Police informants usually have their anonymity protected.

5. Anyone charged with a criminal offence is not required to incriminate himself or herself, has the right to remain silent, and cannot be compelled to be a witness at his or her trial.

EXPERTS

If an expert's opinion is necessary and relevant, if the expert is properly qualified, and if there is no exclusionary rule that would prevent him or her from testifying, the expert's evidence may be admissible.

Necessity

Expert testimony is necessary when it provides information likely to be outside the experience and knowledge of a judge or jury. Consider the example of a woman who is regularly beaten by her spouse. She decides to kill him, fearing that if she does not he will kill her. A layperson might ask why she did not go to the police or to a relative for protection. Clearly, being regularly beaten by a spouse is not part of the average person's experience and knowledge. Without an expert to explain the irrational thought processes common among victims of battered wife syndrome, a judge or jury might be confused about why the woman believed she was acting in self-defence (a defence found in s. 34 of the *Criminal Code*) when she killed her spouse.

Relevance

The expert opinion must be related to a fact in issue, such that the expert opinion is indispensable in coming to a correct understanding of the material elements of the case.

Prejudice Versus Probative Value

For expert testimony to be admitted, its prejudicial effect must be outweighed by its probative value. (The risk of prejudice exists because scientific or medical opinion is often very impressive and difficult to ignore.) For its probative value to be high, the reliability of the body of knowledge on which the expert's testimony is based must be strong. Factors that determine reliability include the extent to which the scientific community accepts the expert's theory or technique, the number and kind of errors the theory or technique can produce, and the care with which the theory or technique has been employed.

Prejudice enters the picture because there is always a great danger that the judge or jurors will be overwhelmed or overawed by the glitter of an expert's experience and knowledge. They may simply accept the expert's opinion and base their judgment solely on the expert's conclusion. The expert's credentials may thus be given exaggerated importance vis-à-vis other evidence (or the absence of evidence) and may lead to faulty conclusions. Another problem may arise if a party does not have the financial resources to hire an expert as impressive as its opponent's to supply a contrary opinion. Experts often have completely opposing views, and their evidence may succeed only in confusing the judge or jury and clouding the real issues.

Properly Qualifying an Expert

voir dire
a hearing in the absence of the jury to consider the admissibility of a piece of evidence

An expert is properly qualified during a ***voir dire*** (a French term meaning "see what is said"). During a *voir dire* the trial itself stops so that the judge can decide an issue of admissibility without the jury being present (the *voir dire* is sometimes called a "trial within the trial"). Once the determination is made, the trial resumes. During the *voir dire* the expert must show that he or she "possesses special knowledge and experience going beyond that of the trier of fact" (Paciocco, 1996, p. 122). It is at this point that the expert must define his or her precise area of expertise. The expert should not be allowed to offer opinion evidence on matters beyond this established expertise. Police officers are sometimes qualified by the courts to give expert opinion evidence—for example, about the street value of illegal drugs or the behaviour of criminal gangs. In these cases, the officer's experience and training (including any special courses taken) will be considered.

SUMMARY

1. Expert testimony is admissible only when it provides information likely to be outside the experience and knowledge of the ordinary judge or jury.

2. Expert evidence can be prejudicial where it tends to overawe a judge or jury, and thus can be given more weight than it deserves.

3. One must have proper credentials to testify as an expert.

PRIOR STATEMENTS

Prior Consistent Statements

Generally, witness statements given to the police that are consistent with the version of events the witnesses describe in court are not admissible. Consider the example of Sally, a friend of the accused who tells the police that she saw him shortly after the crime was committed and that he was upset and had blood on his shirt. When called to testify at trial, she essentially repeats what she told the police. The prosecution is not permitted to introduce her statement to the police, for that would constitute oath helping, an improper attempt to bolster Sally's credibility as a witness. However, if Sally forgets her story and asks to see her statement while she is on the stand, she may be permitted to see it. In fact, police officers often ask to see their notes when testifying so that they can refresh their memory.

A prior consistent statement may also be admissible in the following circumstances:

1. *Recent fabrication*   If the opposing party alleges that a witness has recently concocted his or her story, the prior consistent statement may be admissible to rebut this presumption. Assume, for example, that during a robbery trial a witness alleges that he remembers the accused's "cold blue eyes." On cross-examination defence counsel may suggest that the witness, having seen the accused in court for the first time, has decided to spice up his testimony by alluding to the accused's eye colour. The prosecution will be able to rebut this accusation by referring to the witness's initial statement (containing a reference to blue eye colour) to the police.

2. *The prior consistent statement is part of the narrative*   A need to preserve the witness's narrative by including the witness's prior statements arises most often when the witness is also the victim of the crime. In the case of children's complaints or complaints of

sexual assault, prior statements often help the judge and jury understand what was going on in the mind of the victim immediately after the abuse. This is sometimes called recent complaint. In the past it was thought that a victim of sexual assault bolstered his or her credibility by immediately telling someone about the assault, and hence it was important to admit such statements into evidence. Today, although prior statements may play a role in sexual assault cases, we know much more about how victims react to sexual assault, and we try to avoid the stereotypes of the past.

3. *The prior consistent statement is an exculpatory statement made on arrest* **Exculpatory statements** are statements that provide evidence supporting the accused's innocence. If a suspect makes such a statement at the time of arrest, it is admissible as a prior consistent statement. The idea is that admitting such statements rebuts the inference that someone who is silent on arrest must be guilty. However, exculpatory statements made later, for example at a police station after the suspect is cautioned, are admissible only if the Crown chooses to use them.

exculpatory statement
a statement denying guilt made by the accused

Prior Inconsistent Statements

If a witness tells a story in court different from the one he or she initially told the police, this prior inconsistent statement is not immediately admissible. Sections 9(1) and 9(2) of the *Canada Evidence Act* govern the admissibility of such statements:

> 9(1) A party producing a witness shall not be allowed to impeach his credit by general evidence of bad character, but if the witness, in the opinion of the court, proves adverse, the party may contradict him by other evidence, or, by leave of the court, may prove that the witness made at other times a statement inconsistent with his present testimony, but before the last mentioned proof can be given the circumstances of the supposed statement, sufficient to designate the particular occasion, shall be mentioned to the witness, and he shall be asked whether or not he did make the statement.

> 9(2) Where the party producing a witness alleges that the witness made at other times a statement in writing, [or] reduced to writing ... inconsistent with the witness' present testimony, the court may, without proof that the witness is adverse, grant leave to that party to cross-examine the witness as to the statement and the court may consider the cross-examination in determining whether in the opinion of the court the witness is adverse.

The procedure for bringing such an application, once the inconsistent evidence has been given, is as follows:

1. Counsel informs the court that they are bringing a s. 9(1) or s. 9(2) application.

2. The jury is given a recess and a *voir dire* begins.

3. Counsel then pinpoint the areas of inconsistency between the initial statement and the testimony just given.

4. If the judge agrees that inconsistencies exist, it is up to counsel to prove that the prior statement was made by the witness.

5. The witness is asked whether he or she made the statement. If the witness admits it, the statement is proved; if not, other evidence may be called to prove that it was made (Paciocco, 1996, p. 274).

For the prior statement to be used for the truth of its contents, it must be found to be reliable. This concept was briefly touched on in the discussion of hearsay in chapter 3. It is one thing to introduce a statement simply to impeach the testimony of a witness and make him or her appear less credible, but a much higher threshold of reliability is needed for the statement to be admitted for the truth of its contents. The best indicator of reliability is voluntariness; therefore, it is important to prove that the statement was made voluntarily.

When an oral or written statement is made by a person accused or suspected of a crime to a person in authority, and the prosecution intends to use the statement to incriminate the maker, the prosecution must prove beyond a reasonable doubt that the statement was voluntary before it can be admitted. This test has also been used by the courts with respect to recanting witnesses.

The rationale for proving voluntariness is to ensure the reliability of evidence, especially confession evidence. The idea is that an induced or coerced statement is less credible, and therefore that no threats or inducements will be tolerated. A good example of the problems associated with prior inconsistent statements is found in the popular movie *In the Name of the Father*, which is about a group of young Irishmen and Irishwomen who are accused of being IRA bombers. The police use illegal means to elicit a confession (that is, beatings and psychological abuse). Ultimately the members of the group confess to crimes they did not commit. This is why it is so important to document and videotape police conduct toward an accused; otherwise, the credibility of an accused's statements will be questioned. It is important to remember, as well, that current Canadian law on prior inconsistent statements was first established in the case of David Milgaard. We now know that Milgaard was innocent and that the original witness statements he made to the police were untrue.

SUMMARY

1. A prior consistent statement may be admissible to rebut an allegation of recent fabrication, if it is a necessary part of the narrative, or if it is an exculpatory statement made by the accused on arrest.

2. The admissibility of prior inconsistent statements is governed by ss. 9(1) and 9(2) of the *Canada Evidence Act*.

3. If a prior inconsistent statement is to be admitted for the truth of its contents, the statement must be proved to have been completely voluntary.

THE MECHANICS OF TESTIFYING

Witnesses who are asked to testify can be compelled to come to court when they are served with a subpoena. This means that the witness is legally obligated to attend court. The witness must not only attend court, but must remain in court until the judge officially excuses him or her. Failure to comply with these obligations may result in arrest and a criminal charge. Naturally, if a witness is unable to attend court because of illness or for other serious reasons, no legal repercussions will ensue, as long as the court is notified in advance.

At the beginning of the trial the judge may request that all the witnesses leave the courtroom. Witnesses are then readmitted to the courtroom one by one as they are called to testify. This ensures that witnesses are not influenced by the testimony of others.

Once a witness is called to testify, the court clerk will ask the witness to swear an oath or make an affirmation. If the witness tells a lie while testifying, he or she can be charged with perjury, which has a maximum penalty of 14 years in prison. In addition, witnesses who are uncooperative or disrespectful to the court may receive an immediate conviction for contempt of court.

As mentioned earlier, witnesses are called by either the Crown or the defence, and are referred to as "Crown witnesses" or "defence witnesses," respectively.

The lawyers on both sides have an opportunity to question each witness in the following manner:

examination-in-chief
a party's questioning of its own witnesses

leading question
a question the phrasing of which "suggests" the answer sought

1. *Examination-in-chief*   The witness is questioned first by counsel for his or her side. For example, a Crown witness is questioned first by Crown counsel. On **examination-in-chief** leading questions are not permitted. A **leading question** is one that suggests its answer. "You have a drinking problem, don't you?" is a leading question. "How often do you drink?" would be an acceptable alternative. If counsel have properly prepared their witness, the best style of questioning is simply to let the witness tell his or her story in an uninterrupted narrative. Usually, the witness has been called because he or she can provide information helpful to the calling side's argument. However, witnesses sometimes surprise counsel by changing their story. As discussed above, ss. 9(1) and 9(2) of the *Canada Evidence Act* provide ways in which counsel can treat their witnesses as **adverse** and question them in a manner that is more akin to cross-examination.

adverse witness
a witness called in support of one's own side, but whose evidence turns out to be unfavourable

2. *Cross-examination*   After the examination-in-chief, opposing counsel have an opportunity to question the witness. Unlike examination-in-chief, leading questions are permitted on cross-examination because

the lawyer is attempting to get at information that the witness may be reluctant to recount or does not realize is important. The purposes of cross-examination are to

a. strengthen the questioner's side by weakening the force of the witness's testimony,

b. bring out new information that supports the questioner's side, and

c. discredit the witness.

Cross-examination can be gruelling. Its purpose is to ensure that witnesses are telling the truth and that they are not overstating their evidence or failing to tell the court the whole story. Consider, for example, a witness who is convinced that he or she saw something clearly, and gives evidence to that effect in court. Cross-examination may establish that the witness's view was obstructed or that the witness's eyesight is poor, and thus weaken the impact of the original version. It is important to test evidence this way. That is why evidence that has not been subjected to cross-examination (such as hearsay) has less value or weight than evidence that has. It is important to remember that cross-examination does not always involve an attack. More often, and most effectively, cross-examination brings out new information that did not come out during the examination-in-chief.

3. *Re-examination*   After opposing counsel are finished with the witness, the original examiner has an opportunity to **re-examine** or **re-direct** his or her witness. Re-examination is limited to questions on issues raised for the first time on cross-examination. Because the questioner is again addressing a witness that belongs to his or her side, leading questions are not permitted. The purpose of re-examination is to rebuild testimony that was disturbed by the cross-examination. Assume, for example, that during examination-in-chief the Crown asked its witness to describe a certain person, and the witness said that that person had "a goatee." On cross-examination, however, opposing counsel press the witness into admitting that "it may have been a full beard." On re-examination the Crown would be wise to ask a question such as, "To the best of your recollection, what kind of facial hair did the man have?" The witness would most likely respond by saying, "A goatee," thus reaffirming the witness's original statement.

re-examination/re-direct
a party's questioning of its own witnesses after cross-examination has been completed

At the close of a party's case, the opposing party may bring forward reply or rebuttal evidence to contradict or qualify any new facts or issues that have been raised.

ANSWERING QUESTIONS

In Canada, unlike the United States, witnesses have no right to refuse to answer questions that might incriminate them. Barring a claim of privilege or a successful objection (on the issue of relevance, for example), witnesses must answer all questions posed by Crown or defence counsel or by the judge. Protection against self-incrimination in Canada is provided by the *Canada Evidence Act* and the Charter which ensure that the witness's answers cannot be used against him or her in other proceedings. Thus, even if answering a question involves owning up to criminal behaviour, the witness is bound by his or her oath or affirmation. For example, if Ewan was an eyewitness to the disposal of a body at the waterfront, and during cross-examination defence counsel ask, "What exactly were you doing at the waterfront at 3:00 a.m.?" Ewan would have to answer honestly that he was waiting for a shipment of hashish.

Although s. 5(2) of the *Canada Evidence Act* provides that a witness must answer questions that incriminate him or her, those answers cannot be used in evidence in any criminal trial or other proceeding against him or her. This immunity is also covered by s. 13 of the Charter, which provides that "a witness who testifies in any proceeding has the right not to have any incriminating evidence so given used to incriminate that witness in any other proceedings, except in a prosecution for perjury or for the giving of contradictory evidence." The application of this right is automatic and does not require any claim to protection. Thus, even if Ewan does own up to drug smuggling, this statement cannot be used against him at a later date. Police are not barred, however, from using what they now know about Ewan to gather other evidence concerning his behaviour.

SUMMARY

1. Every witness is subject to questioning by the lawyers for both sides.

2. Leading questions are not permitted during the examination-in-chief or re-examination. However, they are permitted during the cross-examination.

3. Cross-examination is important because it gives the opposing party an opportunity to bring out new information or to weaken the effect of the evidence.

4. A witness must answer all questions posed by counsel, even if the answers tend to incriminate that witness. However, incriminating statements cannot be used against the witness in a later proceeding.

KEY TERMS

competence	compellability
oath	subpoena
solemn affirmation	solicitor–client privilege
unsworn testimony	spousal privilege

public interest and unity privilege   exculpatory statement

police informant privilege   examination-in-chief

agent provocateur   leading question

privilege against self-incrimination   adverse witness

voir dire   re-examination/re-direct

REVIEW

■ TRUE OR FALSE?

_____ 1. Any witness that is competent is also compellable.

_____ 2. Children under age 14 are incompetent to testify.

_____ 3. Unsworn evidence is sometimes admissible.

_____ 4. Common law spouses cannot be forced to testify against one another.

_____ 5. If co-accused are charged on the same information they are not compellable witnesses against each other.

_____ 6. Under no circumstances can a lawyer reveal what the client has told him or her.

_____ 7. Leading questions are not permitted on re-examination.

_____ 8. Using prior consistent statements to bolster a witness's credibility is an example of oath helping.

_____ 9. A recent complaint by a sexual assault victim is admissible.

_____ 10. An agent provocateur is a female undercover police officer.

■ MULTIPLE CHOICE

1. The prosecution may have to reveal the identity of a police informant if

   a. proving the innocence of the accused depends on this information

   b. the informant knows the accused

   c. the defence suspects the identity of the informant

   d. all of the above

2. Spouses may testify against each other if

   a. the offence involves children under age 14

   b. their marriage is failing

   c. the charge concerns indecent acts

   d. all of the above

3. Expert evidence is admissible when

   a. there are not enough witnesses to prove the case without it

   b. both sides can show that they can afford experts of equal authority

   c. an issue that goes beyond the average person's experience must be resolved

   d. the issue of mental capacity is raised

4. A *voir dire* can be characterized as follows:

   a. the court removes itself to a location pertinent to the case

   b. the trial stops to allow the judge to decide an issue in the absence of the jury

   c. when counsel argue an application under s. 9 of the *Canada Evidence Act*

   d. informal discussions between counsel and the judge take place

5. If an accused makes an exculpatory statement on arrest,

   a. the statement usually cannot be admitted, because it violates the rule that prior consistent statements are inadmissible

   b. he or she lacks credibility as a witness

   c. the statement rebuts the inference that guilty people are silent on arrest

   d. the statement will be admissible only if it amounts to a prior inconsistent statement

■ FILL IN THE BLANKS

1. "You loved him, didn't you, Mrs. Banks?" is an example of a _____ question.

2. If a witness does not want to swear on the Bible, he or she may _____.

3. A _____ is usually hand-delivered to people who are required to testify at a trial.

4. An accused has the right not to testify against himself or herself. This right is called the right against _____.

5. _____ protects clients by allowing lawyers to keep their confidences.

6. When the Crown refuses to disclose the identity of an undercover officer, it is claiming the _____ privilege.

7. If the opposing party alleges _____, the other party may introduce evidence of a prior consistent statement.

■ SHORT ANSWER

1. The Crown has no videotape or audiotape of a confession made by an accused. Would the accused's written confession and the officer's notes on the confession be enough to admit the confession for the truth of its contents? Why?

2. If a child does not really understand the moral consequences of the oath, can he or she still testify? What characteristics must the child have to allow him or her to testify?

3. If a client asks his or her lawyer to hide a gun and a bloody shirt, does solicitor–client privilege protect the lawyer's actions?

CHAPTER 6

Legal Rights of Witnesses and of the Accused, and the Implications for Admissibility

CHAPTER OBJECTIVES

After completing this chapter, you should be able to:

◆ Describe the legally appropriate way to interview witnesses.

◆ Explain when a suspect must be cautioned by an officer.

◆ Describe the Charter rights of the accused.

◆ Explain why evidence obtained in violation of Charter rights may be excluded.

QUESTIONING WITNESSES' EVIDENCE WITHOUT INFRINGING THE RIGHTS OF WITNESSES

At the outset of an investigation the most important objective is to gather evidence of any kind. At this stage, the officers are simply attempting to establish the nature of the offence (if there is an offence), corroborate the complaint, establish the suspect's identity, locate the suspect, and establish facts that exceed mere suspicion. Witnesses are the best resources for obtaining this information, and in order to obtain the most complete information available, witness statements should be taken as soon after the incident as possible.

When a police officer is trying to discover whether, or by whom, an offence has been committed, he or she is entitled to question any person, suspect or not, whom he or she thinks can provide useful information. This right applies whether or not the person has been taken into custody, as long as the person has not been charged with the offence or informed that he or she may be prosecuted for it. There is an important distinction, however, between a witness, or a person about whom there are suspicions (a "suspect"), and someone who is about to be arrested.

Although the police cannot force people to answer their questions, deliberate interference with police questioning may result in a charge of obstructing justice under s. 129 of the *Criminal Code*:

Every one who ...

(b) omits, without reasonable excuse, to assist a public officer or peace officer in the execution of his duty in arresting a person or in preserving the peace, after having reasonable notice that he is required to do so, ...

is guilty of

(d) an indictable offence ...

This section does not create an obligation to answer police questions. However, a witness who is reluctant to speak to the police can bring suspicion on himself or herself, whether that suspicion is logical or not. Most people, though, understand the importance of assisting the police.

SUMMARY

1. A police officer is entitled to question any person who may have useful information about an offence, although no one is obliged to answer questions.

WHEN DOES A WITNESS BECOME A SUSPECT OR AN ACCUSED?

The transition from witness to suspect can occur at any time: just after the police arrive at the scene; when the police are taking a statement from the witness; or when another's statement provides a basis for suspicion. The determination that a witness has become a suspect depends on the investigating officer having a reasonable belief that the person has committed the offence under investigation.

This change in status has important implications. For a statement to be admissible in court, it must be proved to have been voluntary. The courts generally require proof that the suspect knew what was being said could be used in court against him or her, and that the statement was made of the suspect's own free will. Accordingly, the suspect should be

cautioning
giving a suspect formal notice of his or her right to freedom from self-incrimination before questioning begins; "reading him his rights"

cautioned. Although there is no set wording for a caution, the following is a good example of one:

You need not say anything. You have nothing to hope from any promise or favour and nothing to fear from any threat, whether or not you say anything. Anything you do say may be used as evidence.

Cautioning a person at the moment that he or she becomes a suspect helps prove the voluntariness of the responses to previous investigative questions as well as responses to any further questions. If the officer continues to question the person after he or she becomes a suspect, without administering a caution, all the answers could be ruled involuntary. It is obvious that unless the suspect understands that he or she is not forced to answer, they may assume they have no choice in the matter, or may be intimidated into answering questions they would not otherwise wish to.

DETENTION AND ARREST

After cautioning the suspect, the officer may simply invite the suspect to accompany him or her to the police station for further questioning. If the suspect refuses, he or she will have to be detained. Detention has considerable significance because the *Canadian Charter of Rights and Freedoms* guarantees the right to counsel (a lawyer) to anyone who is arrested *or* detained. The Charter also guarantees the right to be *informed* about the right to counsel—and the courts have interpreted that to mean the right to be informed immediately. In many situations a suspect will be advised of his or her right to counsel when he or she is cautioned. However, these are separate legal requirements.

Detention has been defined as the restraint of a citizen by a police officer where coercion and compulsion are involved. **Arrest** involves an act by an officer indicating his or her intention to detain or take a person into custody and thereby subject that person to the officer's control and will. Detention is sometimes called **detention short of arrest** or **investigative detention**. For example, when an officer in the RIDE program stops a car and asks the driver to submit to a Breathalyzer test, that person is being detained, not arrested. If that person has a blood alcohol reading over a certain limit, however, the officer will most likely arrest him or her, with the intention of taking him or her into custody.

arrest
detention of a citizen by a police officer combined with an intent to immediately take that person into police custody

detention short of arrest/ investigative detention
the restraint of a person by a police officer (in the absence of an arrest), usually for the purpose of questioning

SUMMARY

1. As soon as a police officer suspects a witness of being the perpetrator of the crime under investigation, the officer must caution that person.

2. Cautioning simply involves telling the suspect that he or she need not say anything, but that anything he or she chooses to say may be given in evidence.

CHARTER RIGHTS OF SUSPECTS AND ACCUSED

The *Canadian Charter of Rights and Freedoms* guarantees accused persons certain rights. If these rights are infringed or denied, evidence can be excluded. The following are the most important rights:

The Right to Counsel

Section 10 of the Charter provides that on arrest *or* detention everyone has the right "to be informed promptly of the reasons therefor" and "to retain and instruct counsel without delay and to be informed of that right."

Thus the first thing the police must do is advise a detainee, in a language that he or she understands (whether that is English or another language) exactly what the right to counsel means. An officer cannot simply repeat a formulaic warning about the right to counsel, but must ensure that the detainee understands this right.

If a suspect requests counsel, the police must stop their questioning. As well, when an accused requests the assistance of counsel, a police officer is under a positive duty to facilitate contact with counsel by giving the accused a reasonable opportunity to exercise his or her right to counsel (through access to a telephone, for example). Further, when the accused expresses a concern that his or her inability to afford a lawyer is an impediment to his or her exercise of the right to counsel, the officer has a duty to tell the accused about the availability of duty counsel and legal aid.

The Right To Remain Silent

The right to remain silent is protected by s. 7 of the Charter and is supported by the privilege against self-incrimination. This right is included in the initial cautioning of the suspect and continues through detention, arrest, and the entire criminal trial process.

The police may question the suspect, and as long as police persuasion does not deny the suspect the right to choose, or deprive him or her of an operating mind, it does not breach the right to silence. The right to silence bars any attempt to bribe the suspect with promises of a lighter sentence, or to subject the suspect to threats (physical or otherwise), but does not affect voluntary statements made to others.

However, the right to silence may be violated when the police subvert the suspect's constitutional right not to make a statement to the authorities. For example, if an accused clearly tells the police that he or she does not wish to make a statement, and then an undercover officer is put in the same cell as the accused and attempts to get his or her cellmate to talk, the accused's right to silence is violated. There is, accordingly, a distinction between the use of undercover agents to observe a suspect, and their use to actively elicit information in violation of the suspect's choice to remain silent (see *R v. Hebert*).

The Right To Be Secure Against Unreasonable Search and Seizure

Section 8 of the Charter protects everyone's right to privacy. There is a very strong tradition in the courts with regard to ensuring privacy, especially as it relates to private dwellings. This tradition owes its origins to ancient property rights, as summarized in the old adage that "an Englishman's home is his castle."

Generally speaking, police officers must have very good reasons to infringe this privacy right. Most often the police wish to gain access to dwelling-houses, other buildings, yards, or cars to search for and obtain evidence of a crime. "Real" evidence such as stolen property or narcotics is often recovered during such searches. There are some circumstances where police may conduct a search without first obtaining a search warrant, but in general a warrant must be obtained for a search to be considered reasonable.

But the search may be unreasonable even when the police obtain a warrant. Consider, for example, that the police obtain a warrant to search 128 Boulevard St., a private dwelling-house, for marijuana said to be growing in the basement with the help of special lights. The warrant specifies the basement. The police locate the plants, but then search other parts of the house. In a corner of the attic they find some obscene materials, which they confiscate. The attic search would be considered unreasonable, for the warrant did not give the police carte blanche to inspect every nook and cranny of the premises. Here the accused's right to be free from unreasonable search and seizure was violated.

SUMMARY

1. Once a suspect is detained or arrested, the officer must inform him or her of the right to counsel.

2. The right to counsel means that the suspect is entitled to be informed of the right and given an opportunity to contact counsel. If the suspect expresses concern about paying for counsel, the officer must also inform the suspect about legal aid.

3. If a suspect expresses interest in obtaining counsel, the officer must cease questioning the suspect until he or she has contacted counsel.

4. A suspect has the right to remain silent, meaning that he or she is never obligated to answer questions asked by the police.

5. Like everyone else, a suspect also has the right to be free from unreasonable search and seizure.

EXCLUSION OF EVIDENCE COLLECTED IN VIOLATION OF RIGHTS

Any evidence that is collected directly or indirectly in violation of an accused's rights may be excluded from the trial. Without the excluded evidence, the prosecution may not be able to prove its case, and thus an accused who could have been found guilty will be acquitted. This frustrating situation may be avoided by scrupulously adhering to the rules governing the collection of evidence.

The Rationale

The fact that we as Canadians pride ourselves on our free and democratic society means that the rights of the most despised and reviled members of our society must be given as much respect as those of the most highly regarded citizens. Our criminal justice system is based on the belief that we would rather see a guilty person walk free than convict an innocent person. Convicting the innocent is a greater harm because it means that not only has an innocent person been terribly harmed, but the real criminal remains free to offend again. Accordingly, the accused is not only presumed innocent, but also receives the benefit of any reasonable doubts raised by the evidence. Mr. Justice Brandeis of the US Supreme Court, in his dissent in *Olmstead* (1928), had this to say:

> In a government of laws, existence of the government will be imperilled if it fails to observe the law scrupulously.
>
> Crime is contagious. If Government becomes a law breaker, it breeds contempt for the law; it invites every man to become a law unto himself; it invites anarchy. To declare that in the administration of criminal justice the end justifies the means—to declare that Government may commit crimes in order to secure the conviction of a private individual—would bring terrible retribution. (p. 485)

This means that state agents—that is, the police—must be held to the highest standard in observing the laws they uphold. They must be especially careful to be faithful to the constitution—the Charter—which is the highest law in Canada. In this way the government, through its agents, becomes a model to be emulated by the citizenry.

The Analytical Steps

Not every breach of a Charter right will result in evidence being excluded. Once a breach of a Charter right has been found, and it has been determined that evidence was obtained as a result of the breach, the issue of exclusion must still be addressed, in accordance with s. 24(2) of the Charter. The issues of whether a Charter right has been breached and whether the evidence will be excluded are normally addressed in a *voir dire*.

Step One

The analysis of whether evidence was gathered improperly begins by asking whether the accused has established, on a balance of probabilities, that evidence was obtained as a result of a breach, denial, or infringement of a Charter right. The analysis proceeds as follows:

1. *Identify the specific Charter right*   For example, was a denial of the right to counsel involved?

2. *Demonstrate a breach of that right*   For example, did the accused repeatedly ask to see a lawyer, and did the police respond by continuing their questioning instead of helping him or her obtain counsel?

3. *Demonstrate that the breach of the Charter right resulted in the obtaining of evidence*   For example, did the accused give in to the police and make a confession after they refused to help the accused obtain

counsel? Note that the link between the breach and the evidence does not need to be direct.

The above analysis includes a two-part inquiry:

1. *Prima facie breach of a Charter right*   The burden is on the applicant—that is, the defence—to show that there was at least a *prima facie* violation of the accused's Charter rights.

2. *Justification*   After the defence has made its *prima facie* case, the Crown is allowed to demonstrate that in the circumstances the police acted in a reasonable manner. For example, if the accused was denied the right to counsel while detained or arrested, the Crown could demonstrate that the accused did not intend to exercise the right, or insisted on a lawyer who was out of town, or would not settle for advice from duty counsel when the investigation was pressing.

Step Two

If the judge finds that a Charter breach occurred, the question of exclusion is then addressed. (If the judge finds that no Charter breach occurred, the *voir dire* is over and the evidence is admissible.) The crucial question in determining whether evidence should be excluded is, could the admission of the evidence bring the administration of justice into further disrepute? A three-part test (see below) determines whether admission of the evidence could bring the administration of justice into further disrepute (that is, weaken or be perceived as weakening the integrity of the justice system's commitment to the values expressed in the Charter).

Section 24(2) is not designed to be a tool to control or discipline police conduct, and therefore one must establish more than police misconduct to exclude the evidence. The arbiter of how the administration of justice would be affected by the admission of evidence is the somewhat artificial legal construct of "the well-informed member of the community." This ideal person is to decide whether, depending on the seriousness of the breach and the impact on trial fairness, it would be more detrimental to include the evidence at the expense of Charter values, or to exclude the evidence and possibly release a guilty person back into society.

The Three-Part Test

1. *Trial unfairness*   Denial of freedom from self-incrimination is, at least on first impression, unfair. Thus in most cases where infringement or denial of a Charter right results in self-incriminating evidence (usually a confession), the evidence will be excluded. If violation of a Charter right results in the obtaining of "real" evidence, the impact on the individual may not be considered to be as unfair, for there is always the possibility that "real" evidence will be discovered anyway.

2. *Seriousness of the breach*   Technical, trivial, or inadvertent breaches should not result in the exclusion of evidence. This is the step where the exclusion of "real" evidence is most often analyzed, such as drugs or weapons. These are less likely to be excluded unless the Charter violation is very serious.

3. *Effect of exclusion*   The question is whether it would cause more disrepute to exclude than to admit the evidence. Community values are assessed at this point to aid in determining the impact on the justice system's reputation.

SUMMARY

1. Evidence that is obtained as a result of a breach of a Charter right ought to be excluded because it violates the fairness of the trial and brings the administration of justice into disrepute.

2. The procedure for determining whether a piece of evidence should be excluded is governed by s. 24(2) of the Charter.

3. Technical or trivial breaches will not result in evidence being excluded, but a blatant disregard for the rights enshrined in the Charter will definitely result in exclusion.

KEY TERMS

cautioning

arrest

detention short of arrest/
investigative detention

REVIEW

■ TRUE OR FALSE?

_____ 1. Statements should be taken as soon after an incident as possible.

_____ 2. Every witness must be cautioned before being interviewed.

_____ 3. Detention and arrest amount to the same thing.

_____ 4. After a suspect has been told that he or she has the right to instruct counsel, the officer is under no further obligation regarding this right.

_____ 5. The right to remain silent is an extension of the initial cautioning of the accused.

____ **6.** Obtaining a warrant ensures that the police will not violate s. 8 of the Charter.

____ **7.** All evidence that has been obtained as a result of a violation of the Charter will be excluded.

____ **8.** State agents are sometimes allowed to work outside the law.

____ **9.** The Charter is the highest law in Canada.

■ MULTIPLE CHOICE

1. The right to counsel is violated when

   a. a suspect says, "But I have no money for a lawyer," and the officer continues to question the suspect

   b. a suspect who speaks English with difficulty offers no response whatsoever when he or she is informed of the right to counsel

   c. the accused, on trying to call a lawyer, reports that the line is busy and that he or she will call later, yet the officer continues questioning the accused

   d. all of the above

2. Evidence may be excluded from a trial when

   a. the evidence, if admitted, would bring the administration of justice into disrepute

   b. the evidence was obtained during a search and seizure operation

   c. the court learns that the accused declined his or her right to speak with counsel before speaking with the investigating officers

   d. all of the above

■ FILL IN THE BLANKS

1. Evidence may be excluded if it is likely to bring the administration of justice into _____.

2. As soon as a witness becomes a suspect, the officer must _____ the suspect.

3. Detention short of arrest is also known as _____.

■ **SHORT ANSWER**

1. Why is it important for an investigating officer to be aware of the point at which a witness becomes a "suspect"?

2. Did the police act correctly in this scenario? Why?

    Officer: You have the right to instruct counsel, OK?

    Suspect: Yeah … what's that?

    Officer: Do you want to talk to a lawyer?

    Suspect: Dunno … (muttering).

    Officer: Fine. Well. What were you doing in the park? Eh?

3. What is the rationale behind excluding evidence that is obtained in violation of the Charter? Whose interests are being protected?

CHAPTER 7

Respecting Rights in the Collection of Evidence: Searches, Warrants, and Wiretaps

CHAPTER OBJECTIVES

After completing this chapter, you should be able to:

◆ Describe the types of searches that do not require warrants.

◆ Explain how to obtain search warrants and describe when they are needed.

◆ Describe how to execute a warrant.

◆ Define "wiretapping" and describe how to obtain an authorization to wiretap.

SEARCHES

As discussed in chapter 6, s. 8 of the *Canadian Charter of Rights and Freedoms* provides that "everyone has the right to be secure against unreasonable search or seizure"; evidence collected in violation of this right will likely be excluded. Searching and seizing, however, is one of the best ways to collect evidence of a crime. If a police officer has information that a crime is occurring, is about to occur, or has occurred at a certain address or in a certain area, the officer will of course want to pursue this lead by searching the address or area. On the other hand, the need to search for criminals and objects of crime must be balanced against the individual's right to privacy. As was noted in chapter 6, the tradition of respecting privacy rights is a strong one, with solid support in the courts.

WARRANTLESS SEARCHES

A warrantless search is presumed to be unreasonable—that is, it is presumptively unreasonable. The party seeking to justify the search has the opportunity, however, to rebut the presumption. There are a few situations in which warrants are usually not required: when the search is statutorily authorized, when exigent circumstances exist, when the search is incident to arrest, and when the person consents to the search.

Statutorily Authorized Search

An example of a statutorily authorized search power is found in the *Highway Traffic Act*, which authorizes impromptu motor vehicle searches to check for proper insurance and registration as well as for any kind of driver impairment. However, the ability to pull cars over and detain them does not give the police general investigative authority. As with any search, an officer must be able to justify his or her actions as reasonable. In the absence of reasonable and probable grounds for conducting a search, such as the presence of drugs, alcohol, or weapons in **plain view**, any evidence flowing from such a search (including answers to police questions about the drugs or whatever), will be the result of a Charter breach and ought not to be admitted. Assume, for example, that an officer pulls over a car and asks to see the vehicle registration and licence. The driver produces these, but the officer then proceeds to order everyone out of the car and, having no reasonable grounds to do so, checks underneath the seat cushions and in the trunk. The officer discovers a marijuana cigarette butt in the ashtray and seizes it. Because this would be an unreasonable search and seizure, the cigarette would most likely be excluded as evidence.

plain view doctrine
an accepted legal rule that prohibits warrantless searches unless the searching officer has first discovered illegal evidence in plain view

The minimum requirements that must be satisfied for a warrantless vehicle search to be found reasonable are as follows:

1. *Vehicle stopped or the occupants lawfully detained in accordance with a statutory right*   This means that the police are simply checking vehicle registration or for driver impairment, and doing so in a routine, random manner.

2. *When the police have reasonable and probable grounds (RPG) of commission of an offence*   Assume that an officer has information that a robbery suspect driving a gray Ford Taurus is headed north on Spadina Avenue. The officer spots a car fitting that description and pulls it over to search for stolen goods. This is an example of RPG. Another example might be as follows: an officer pulls a car over for a routine check, and when the driver opens the window the officer notices a strong smell of burnt marijuana. The officer then has RPG to search the car for the origin of that odour.

3. *Exigent (emergency) circumstances*   An example of extreme circumstances that would enable an officer to search a car without reasonable and probable grounds for a search might occur when young children have been abducted and the police have set up roadblocks to catch the abductors.

One important consideration in determining the reasonableness of a search is its scope in relation to the offence and the evidence sought. For example, if human life or safety is involved the courts will tolerate a much more invasive search than if the search is simply for soft drugs.

Exigent Circumstances

Section 487.11 of the *Criminal Code* provides that where conditions exist that would justify granting a warrant, but it is impractical to obtain one, an officer may proceed with a search. "Impractical" generally means that time does not allow for applying for a warrant. In most cases, **exigent circumstances** must be present to justify such a search. Exigent circumstances may include the preservation of human life or safety, or the prevention of immediate loss or destruction of evidence.

exigent circumstances
urgent and pressing circumstances (that may justify a warrantless search)

Consider, for example, an officer conducting surveillance of a dwelling-house in an attempt to gather enough evidence for a search warrant. The occupant is suspected of child abduction, but at this point the police simply do not have enough evidence to arrest the suspect or apply for a search warrant. While sitting in his cruiser the officer hears a scream and sees a hand banging on the basement window. He jumps out of the car and, after announcing himself, forcibly enters the dwelling through the front door. In these circumstances the officer clearly has reasonable and probable grounds. He could have obtained a warrant, but time did not allow him to do so, for the preservation of human life or safety was at stake.

Some factors that bear on the reasonableness of protective measures are

1. The nature of the apprehended risk.

2. The potential consequences of not taking protective measures.

3. The probability of the contemplated danger actually occurring.

Search Incident to Arrest

The common law power of **search incident to arrest** gives an officer the authority to search a person on arrest. This power does not extend beyond protecting the arresting officer from armed or dangerous suspects and preserving evidence that may go out of existence or otherwise be lost.

search incident to arrest
a warrantless personal search that is permitted at the time of arrest

For example, if an officer arrests a man for suspected sexual assault, the officer is authorized to frisk him to ensure that he is not carrying weapons and so forth, but is not permitted to start pulling out the suspect's hair for DNA analysis, because hair is not evidence that may go out of existence or otherwise be lost on arrest.

The power of search incident to arrest is discretionary, and an officer can properly choose not to search an individual. But whenever an officer does decide to use the search power, he or she must not conduct the search in an abusive manner. The degree of intrusiveness of the search in the circumstances will be considered by the court in decisions on admissibility. For example, in some circumstances a frisk may be considered reasonable whereas a cavity search may be considered extreme. Assume that airport customs officials have found a small baggie of cocaine in a passenger's carry-on luggage. The passenger is arrested and the police perform a search incident to arrest in which they strip-search the individual and conduct a **cavity search**—that is, explore his rectal cavity. In the circumstances this type of invasive search may be considered unreasonable and result in the baggie that was found by the customs officials being excluded as evidence.

cavity search
a search of the internal body cavities (mouth, vagina, etc.) of a suspect

Consent Search

consent search
a warrantless search that has been expressly permitted by the person (or the person in control of the private property) being searched

A **consent search** is a search in which the police have obtained the permission of the person being searched and thus do not need any other authorization to perform the search. In effect, this means that the person being searched has waived his or her s. 8 Charter right against unreasonable search or seizure. Such a waiver of s. 8 (or any Charter right) requires

1. Consent, express or implied.

2. The authority to give consent.

3. Voluntariness (consent that is not the product of oppression).

4. Awareness of the nature of the police conduct to which consent is given.

5. Awareness of the right to refuse consent.

6. Awareness of the potential consequences of giving consent.

Thus the police must be absolutely certain that the suspect understands the rights he or she is relinquishing. In certain circumstances the police do not have to inform the accused of the right to refuse consent as long as the accused is sufficiently aware of his or her rights. To be on the safe side, however, under normal circumstances the police should inform the accused that he or she has the right to refuse consent, and that to relinquish the right means the loss of his or her right to complain should the police find evidence of an offence. Consider the following conversation:

Officer: We are going to search your apartment now, OK?

Woman: Well, my boyfriend's not here right now, and it's his place. Maybe you could come back another time?

Officer: Oh, that's OK, we won't be long.

Woman: I'm really not sure …

Officer: Really, it's OK. We'll be out of here in 15 minutes.

Although the woman in this example never actually says no, clearly this dialogue is fraught with problems. First of all, the woman does not have the authority to consent: it is not her apartment. Second, she seems to be unaware of the consequences of permitting a search. Finally, the officer appears to be bullying her into complying. Should the officer find evidence of an offence in this apartment, it will most likely never be admitted in court.

SUMMARY

1. Because our right to privacy is so well guarded, a search without a warrant is presumed to be unreasonable.

2. However, warrantless searches may be acceptable when

   a. they are statutorily authorized,

   b. there are exigent circumstances,

   c. the search is incident to arrest, or

   d. the consent of the person being searched is obtained.

WARRANTS

When in doubt, an officer should obtain a warrant before conducting a search. There are many types of warrants, and the type applied for depends on the type of search required. The two most useful types of warrants, as far as evidence gathering is concerned, are

1. general warrants (under s. 487.01 of the *Criminal Code*), and

2. DNA warrants (under ss. 487.04-487.09 of the *Criminal Code*).

General Warrants

The purpose of a **general warrant** is to enable the police to enter premises for the purpose of locating items that will be used as evidence that a crime has been committed.

general warrant
a court-sanctioned grant of permission to search a stipulated location for the purpose of collecting evidence

Section 487(1) of the *Criminal Code* provides that a search warrant may be issued for the seizure of

(a) anything relating to an offence which has been or is suspected to have been committed against the Code or any other Act of Parliament,

(b) anything that is reasonably believed will be evidence of an offence against the Code or any other Act of Parliament, or

(c) anything that is reasonably believed to be intended to be used to commit an offence against the person, for which the offender may be arrested without a warrant.

Warrants may be issued for a building, a receptacle (container), or a "place." A warrant must narrowly define a place because of the gravity of infringing on the important right of privacy. The definition of place includes fixed locations such as offices, shops, and gardens, as well as vehicles, vessels, and aircraft, but does not include public streets or other public places. Consider the example of a person who informs the police that he has seen his neighbour photographing naked children in the shed behind the neighbour's house. Given this information, the officer in charge should request a warrant only for the shed, *not* for the house and the rest of the neighbour's property. Police officers should not be searching places for which there are no reasonable and probable grounds for a search. A hunch or suspicion is not enough.

Procedure

To obtain a warrant, an "information" must be sworn on oath before a justice of the peace. The information is simply a document in which the officer describes a set of facts, usually based on a tip from an informant. The information must provide the name of the suspect or owner of the area to be searched, the address to be searched, a description of the informant (which may or may not reveal his or her identity), a description of the suspected offence, and a list of articles to be searched for. The warrant must be very specific, for an officer cannot expect a warrant to license wanton ransacking. The items to be searched for must be readily identifiable—for example, "needles and scales," not "drug paraphernalia." If the wording is found to be overly vague by the court, the validity of the search warrant may be attacked and the warrant quashed (meaning the evidence obtained from the warrant will be excluded).

However, if the officer conducting the search happens to notice an illegal substance or object in plain view, he or she may seize it, even though it is not listed in the warrant. This is called the plain view doctrine. Plain view means, for example, in an open bag, not under a sofa or in a closet. The item must be something that the officer has observed during a proper search—that is, a search for the items and of the areas outlined in the warrant itself.

The information should also set out in detail the offence for which the items are being sought. The officer who is swearing to the contents of the warrant must also offer reasonable grounds for believing that the items are in the area specified. The officer cannot simply rely on the justice of the peace to ensure that the information in a warrant justifies a search, for justices of the peace are often criticized for granting warrants too lightly, where reasonable grounds are lacking. An officer must take note of the high standards the courts look for when they examine the validity of warrants—after the evidence has already been gathered. It is much worse for an officer to see his or her hard work go to waste in court than to have a little patience and build up the grounds for belief by relying on other investigative techniques before applying for a search warrant.

It is essential that officers be completely truthful when swearing an information before a justice. If an officer misleads the justice in any way, the warrant will be considered defective and the search will be considered warrantless. Consider, for example, an officer who exaggerates facts, such as the number of times a police informant has been used, to impress on a justice just how reliable the officer believes the information to be. This is an unacceptable tactic and will probably result in exclusion of the evidence.

Execution of the Warrant

1. The officer must carry the warrant and produce it on request by those whose premises are being searched.

2. The officer must make a formal demand to be admitted. If the demand is refused, he or she is entitled to break into the premises, but will be liable for the results of excessive force (meaning that if the officer damages the door or any other property more than is necessary to enter, the owner of the property may sue the officer).

3. The right to search people found on the premises exists only if the officer arrests them first. An exception to this rule is found in s. 11(5) of the *Controlled Drug and Substance Act*, which authorizes the police to search anyone suspected of having a controlled drug or substance on his or her person, without the need to arrest.

4. Police are entitled to conduct "reasonable surveillance" of the people whose premises are being searched. However, they are not authorized in all circumstances to detain the occupants during the search.

5. The officers may seize any article named in the warrant and anything that has been obtained by or been used in the commission of an offence, if it is in plain view of the officers.

6. Once the search is completed, the officer must make a report to the justice of the peace who issued the warrant or bring the seized objects before the justice.

7. Section 489.1 of the *Criminal Code* imposes a duty on officers to return any property seized to the person lawfully entitled to possess the property, as long as it is not required as evidence.

DNA Warrants

Sections 487.04-487.09 of the *Criminal Code* set out the procedure for obtaining a **DNA warrant**, which enables police officers to obtain DNA samples from suspects. Consider the example of the sexual assault and murder of a young woman, Cynthia, whose vagina was found to contain semen. Peter, the last person seen with Cynthia, was seen sneaking off into the woods with her after a bush party. His mother recalls that he came home the next morning wet and bedraggled, with his clothes torn. Clearly Peter is the prime suspect. The police arrest him and wish to see whether his DNA matches that found in Cynthia's body. Before the enactment of ss. 487.04-487.09, there was essentially no legal way to obtain blood, hair follicles, or buccal swabs (mouth swabs) directly from a suspect

DNA warrant
a specialized warrant permitting the collection of DNA evidence from the body of a suspect

without his or her consent. Obtaining such samples would have been considered a violation of the suspect's right against self-incrimination. These *Criminal Code* provisions may at some point be subject to a Charter challenge, but for now they exist.

The procedure for obtaining a DNA warrant is similar to the procedure for a general warrant, insofar as the officer must swear to an information in which reasonable and probable grounds are given to support the proposition that a suspect's DNA is likely to match the perpetrator's DNA. The gravity of the bodily intrusion is underlined by the fact that the warrant must be authorized by a judge instead of simply a justice of the peace. Section 487.05(1) provides that

> A provincial court judge who on *ex parte* application is satisfied by information on oath that there are reasonable grounds to believe
> (a) that a designated offence has been committed,
> (b) that a bodily substance has been found
> > (i) at the place where the offence was committed,
> > (ii) on or within the body of the victim of the offence,
> > (iii) on anything worn or carried by the victim at the time when the offence was committed, or
> > (iv) on or within the body of any person or thing or at any place associated with the commission of the offence,
> (c) that a person was a party to the offence, and
> (d) that forensic DNA analysis of a bodily substance from the person will provide evidence about whether the bodily substance referred to in paragraph (b) was from that person
> and who is satisfied that it is in the best interests of the administration of justice to do so may issue a warrant ... authorizing a peace officer to obtain ... a bodily substance from that person.

Section 487.06(1) provides that the only "bodily substances" that may be collected are individual hairs (including the root sheath), epithelial cells (by swabbing the lips, tongue, and inside cheeks), and blood (by pricking the skin surface with a sterile lancet). In addition, before any substance is removed from a suspect, the officer must inform the suspect why the police want to obtain such a sample. The officer must also explain the nature of the procedure and the possibility that the sample will be used as evidence. The statute also provides that all necessary force may be used, and that for the purposes of the warrant a suspect who is not already under arrest may be detained no longer than is reasonable (often, however, the suspect is already in custody). Sections 487.08 and 487.09 also provide for the destruction of the sample if it does not match the perpetrator's DNA, and guarantee that if it does match, it will be used only for investigative purposes.

Telewarrants

telewarrant
a warrant obtained through an expedited process over the telephone

It is sometimes possible to obtain a warrant by telephone; this is called a **telewarrant**. Section 487.01(7) of the *Criminal Code* provides that a police officer may obtain a search warrant from a judicial officer by telephone or other telecommunication when he believes that an indictable offence has been committed.

Procedure

1. To apply for a search warrant by telephone, a police officer must believe that it is impractical to appear personally before a justice of the peace.

2. Application is made by submitting an information on oath by telephone or other telecommunication to the justice, who is required to record it verbatim. The justice then certifies the record of the information (with respect to time, date, and contents) and files it with the clerk of the territorial division in which the warrant is intended for execution. The officer will have to file a similar document after the search has been executed.

This abbreviated procedure is clearly helpful in cases where the officer believes that there is a likelihood the suspect will flee with the evidence before a formal warrant can be issued. However, the same high standard of reasonable and probable grounds that applies to formal warrants must be present before a telewarrant can be issued.

SUMMARY

1. A general warrant is used to gain access to buildings, receptacles, and other "places."

2. A DNA warrant is used to obtain samples of bodily substances from suspected perpetrators in cases where DNA-identifying material was left at a crime scene.

3. To obtain a warrant, the officer in charge needs substantial grounds for belief. The warrant must be authorized by either a judge or a justice of the peace.

4. Telewarrants may be issued over the telephone in certain circumstances.

WIRETAPPING

Wiretapping is the use of technological means to intercept (listen in on) private telephone conversations. Such an interception of private communications by agents of the state without prior judicial authorization constitutes an unreasonable search and seizure that violates s. 8 of the Charter, even if it is consensual.

Applying for a wiretap authorization is covered under s. 185 of the *Criminal Code* and is considerably more stringent than applying for many other kinds of warrants. Wiretap authorizations may be granted only by

wiretapping
the use of technological means to intercept (listen in on) private telephone conversations

a judge of a superior court of criminal jurisdiction. In Ontario, this means a judge of the Ontario Court, General Division. Because wiretapping is a very serious invasion of privacy, it is an investigative technique of last resort.

For such a wiretap authorization to be granted, a judge must be satisfied that

1. the authorization would be in the best interests of justice, and

2. other investigative measures have been tried and failed, or are unlikely to succeed.

The requirements for interceptions intended to prevent bodily harm are set out in s. 184.1(1) of the *Criminal Code*:

> An agent of the state may intercept, by means of any electro-magnetic, acoustic, mechanical or other device, a private communication if
>
> (a) either the originator of the private communication or the person intended by the originator to receive it has consented to the interception;
>
> (b) the agent of the state believes on reasonable grounds that there is a risk of bodily harm to the person who consented to the interception; and
>
> (c) the purpose of the interception is to prevent the bodily harm.

The contents of a private communication that is obtained from such an interception are inadmissible as evidence except for the purposes of proceedings in which actual, attempted, or threatened bodily harm is alleged (s. 184.1(2) of the *Criminal Code*). Section 184.1(3) states that "The agent of the state who intercepts a private communication ... shall, as soon as is practicable in the circumstances, destroy any recording of the private communication that is obtained from an interception ... , any full or partial transcript of the recording and any notes made by that agent of the private communication if nothing in that private communication suggests that bodily harm, attempted bodily harm or threatened bodily harm has occurred or is likely to occur."

Application for a Wiretap Authorization

The procedure is set out in s. 184.2(2) and is similar to an application for a warrant. The officer must prepare an affidavit (sworn statement) stating the following: that there are reasonable grounds to believe an offence against the *Criminal Code* or any other act of Parliament has been or will be committed; the particulars of the offence; the name of the person who has consented to the interception; the period for which the authorization is requested; and, in the case of an application for an authorization where an authorization has previously been granted under s. 184 or s. 186, the particulars of the previous authorization.

Here is an example of a situation where wiretapping might be authorized: Tim has threatened over the telephone on repeated occasions to kill Jane, his ex-girlfriend. On these occasions he cries and ends his calls with threats such as, "If you continue seeing this other guy, I'm going to kill you both." If Jane consents to the police wiretapping her line, there is a good chance that the police will obtain an authorization from a General Division judge, for Jane's safety may be at stake.

SUMMARY

1. In Ontario an authorization for wiretapping must be signed by a General Division judge.

2. Other investigative techniques must be unsuccessful or unlikely to succeed before wiretapping will be authorized.

3. Wiretapping is authorized only to prevent bodily harm.

KEY TERMS

plain view doctrine

exigent circumstances

search incident to arrest

cavity search

consent search

general warrant

DNA warrant

telewarrant

wiretapping

REVIEW

■ TRUE OR FALSE?

_____ 1. Warrantless searches are presumptively reasonable.

_____ 2. Regardless of whether the officer has a warrant, any illegal substance in plain view may be seized.

_____ 3. Statutory permission to conduct a warrantless search does not give the officer carte blanche.

_____ 4. A search incident to arrest includes the dwelling-house of the arrested person.

_____ 5. For someone to truly consent to a search, he or she must be aware of all the consequences of relinquishing one's s. 8 rights.

_____ 6. A general search warrant enables an officer to take buccal swabs.

_____ 7. Where the wording of a search warrant is too vague, the warrant may be considered unreasonable.

_____ 8. A DNA warrant may be authorized by a justice of the peace.

_____ 9. Warrants may be issued over the telephone.

_____ 10. An application for a wiretap is more easily granted than a general warrant.

■ MULTIPLE CHOICE

1. To obtain a wiretap authorization, one needs

   a. physical evidence that someone will suffer bodily harm

   b. proof that all other investigative techniques have been tried and have failed

   c. to demonstrate that other investigative techniques have been unsuccessful or are unlikely to succeed

   d. to demonstrate one's ability to operate an electromagnetic interceptor

2. Bodily substances may be obtained from a suspect or an accused only when

   a. the investigating officer has reasonable and probable grounds to believe that the person is guilty

   b. a DNA warrant has been obtained from a judge

   c. exigent circumstances exist

   d. all of the above

3. An invalid warrant may lead to

   a. the investigating officer being disciplined

   b. the accused being convicted of a lesser offence

   c. disciplinary action against the justice of the peace who approved the warrant

   d. exclusion of evidence at trial

4. If an officer making a routine check of a motor vehicle can clearly see a prohibited weapon, he or she is authorized to

   a. telephone the office for a telewarrant

   b. seize the weapon as evidence

   c. follow the procedures governing searches in exigent circumstances

   d. revoke the car owner's licence

■ FILL IN THE BLANKS

1. The power to conduct searches and find important evidence must be balanced against the individual's _____.

2. _____ are statutorily authorized.

3. Officers may seize items not listed in a search warrant if those items are in _____.

4. In a serious situation involving bodily harm, _____ may justify a warrantless search.

5. A frisk is less invasive than a _____.

6. If a person is prepared to relinquish his or her s. 8 Charter rights, an officer may be permitted to conduct a _____.

7. A wiretap authorization may be signed only by a _____.

■ SHORT ANSWER

1. Does an officer have the right to search people found on the premises during the execution of a search warrant?

2. What are the three bodily substances that may be obtained if an officer has a DNA warrant?

3. Describe a situation in which a wiretap authorization may be granted.

4. If a warrant identified "any illegal drug substances" as the items to be seized, how would the courts react to such a description? What would be the outcome regarding the admissibility of the evidence?

CHAPTER 8

Interviews, Statements, and Confessions

CHAPTER OBJECTIVES

After completing this chapter, you should be able to:

◆ Describe how to interview an accused.

◆ Explain the importance of voluntariness in taking a statement from an accused.

◆ Define the term "inducements."

INTERVIEWING THE ACCUSED

As discussed in chapter 6, as soon as an officer suspects that a witness may have committed the offence being investigated, the witness (now a suspect) must be cautioned—that is, must be told that he or she need not say anything, but if he or she chooses to speak, what is said may be given in evidence. If the officer has sufficient, reasonable, and probable grounds for suspicion, the suspect should be arrested and informed of his or her rights. The most important right at this stage is the right to speak to a lawyer. If the suspect (now an accused) shows an interest in speaking to counsel, the officers are not allowed to question the accused until counsel have arrived and spoken to the accused.

After the accused has refused his or her right to counsel, or consulted a lawyer, the police may resume questioning him or her. If the accused makes a determined effort not to say anything, the police may not employ trickery to induce him or her to speak, for this would violate the right to remain silent.

It is at this point that the accused may choose to confess to the offence for which he or she has been arrested.

CONFESSIONS

The common law rule is that a **confession**—a statement (oral or written) made to a **person in authority** by an accused or someone suspected of a crime, which the authorities intend to use to incriminate the statement

confession
a voluntary statement by an accused, to a person in authority, that is intended to incriminate the accused

person in authority
a person who is involved in the prosecution of the accused, and whom the accused perceives as having authority over the course of the prosecution

105

maker—must be proved beyond a reasonable doubt to have been voluntary before it can be admitted.

A person in authority is anyone who was or is involved in the arrest, detention, examination, or prosecution of the accused, and who is perceived by the accused as having authority or control over him or her, or over the course of the prosecution. This definition has been considered broad enough to encompass people such as the parents of an accused who act in the presence of or under the directions of a person in authority (such as a police officer). This type of third-party involvement usually takes the form of a party acting as a go-between by informing the accused about **inducements** offered by the person in authority. These third parties will have their conduct questioned or examined to ensure that no threats were made or inducements offered. If a parent is in the interrogation room saying, "You better tell the truth, Junior, or I'll beat you black and blue," while a police officer looks on, his or her conduct will be considered as unacceptable as coercion by a person in authority, for the parent is offering an inducement with, it seems, the blessing of the person in authority. (Under the right circumstances, even a victim may be considered an agent of a person in authority.)

inducements
promises, favours, threats, or representations made to the accused that may be perceived as efforts to coerce the accused into making a confession

A statement made to a person not "in authority" is not subject to the rules of admissibility described above. For example, if an accused person says something to a neighbour or a friend, what was said may be admitted as evidence without undergoing the scrutiny that statements to persons in authority would undergo.

The procedure for admitting confessions operates through a *voir dire*. The steps are as follows:

1. The burden of proving that a statement is voluntary is on the prosecution, which must prove voluntariness beyond a reasonable doubt.

2. The test is that the statement must be proved to have been made without threats or inducements, and not in an atmosphere of oppression, and furthermore to have been the product of an operating mind.

3. Once the confession is proved to have been voluntary, and is thus admissible, the Crown has the discretion to determine when or if the statement will be used at trial. Accordingly, if the statement is exculpatory (a denial of guilt), the Crown need not introduce it.

When the statement is an admission of guilt, the Crown will introduce it for its truth as part of the Crown's case in chief. If the statement is a provable lie, the Crown will use it to cross-examine the accused and damage his or her credibility.

Because of the rule that prior consistent statements are inadmissible, the defence may not introduce the statement unless the defence is rebutting an allegation of recent fabrication. That is, if the Crown suggests during its cross-examination of the accused that the accused is making a recently fabricated or concocted defence, defence counsel are permitted to introduce the statement made to the police to demonstrate prior consistency.

Rationale

The rationale behind the confession rule is that statements which are induced or coerced are not worthy of credit. It is presumed that people are capable of saying anything to avoid punishment from authority figures. Another reason why involuntary confessions should not be admissible is that they negatively affect the fairness of the trial. This idea of fairness is linked to the right to remain silent and to the **privilege against self-incrimination**. That is, to convict oneself out of one's own mouth is inherently unfair unless one is clearly volunteering to do so. Fairness implies playing by the rules, and if the police exceed these rules the two sides in the criminal justice system are no longer equally balanced. The last rationale is that the integrity of the trial is affected. The courts believe that they should not ally themselves with improper conduct by the police, and thus believe they are compelled to exclude improperly obtained evidence.

privilege against self-incrimination
a privilege exempting the accused from the obligation to give self-incriminating evidence (or any evidence at all)

SUMMARY

1. To be admissible, a statement made by an accused to a person in authority must be proved beyond a reasonable doubt to have been voluntary.

2. A person in authority can be anyone involved in the arrest or detention of the accused. However, there are persons in authority who fall outside this category.

3. The procedure for admitting confessions is determined on a *voir dire*.

4. The rationale behind the confession rule is that involuntary statements are not reliable evidence.

THE IMPORTANCE OF VOLUNTARINESS

The acquisition of evidence by means of a statement taken by a police officer violates s. 7 of the *Canadian Charter of Rights and Freedoms* and the confession rule only if the manner in which it is acquired infringes on the accused's right to remain silent. If an accused has been informed of his or her right to counsel, there is nothing to stop the police from continuing to question the accused about the offence in a reasonable manner. Should the accused decide to answer these questions and make a statement, it must be completely of his or her own volition. In each case, in order to avoid any allegation of coercion, the court will seek to determine whether there is a causal link between the conduct of the officer and the making of the statement by the accused. Factors to be considered in making this determination include the nature of the exchange and the relationship between the accused and the officer.

Examples of actions by officers that may be considered inducements to confess include

1. Violence or threats of violence.

2. Prolonged interrogation, to the point where the accused might, because of fatigue, suffer a loss of judgment.

3. Threats of the imposition of greater charges, or promises to drop (or substitute less serious) charges; intimidation.

4. The wearing of sidearms (which may be considered a form of intimidation).

Trickery, deception, or any form of lying to the accused may also invalidate a confession. An example would be where an investigator falsely tells an accused that his co-accused has made certain statements that make the accused's claim of innocence a lost cause, and thus that the accused might as well confess. Another example would be where an investigator tells a suspect that his or her fingerprints were found all over the crime scene, when in fact they were not.

In addition, because an admissible statement must be the product of an operating mind, understanding the state of mind of the accused at the time the statement was taken is crucial to a correct determination of voluntariness. If the accused was drunk when the statement was made, or in shock as a result of a motor vehicle collision, the drunkenness or shock become elements for consideration by a judge on a *voir dire*. Since the most commonly encountered problems relating to state of mind are intoxication and impairment, investigators in such situations must make detailed and accurate notes concerning an accused's condition at the time of taking his or her statement. In major crime investigations where state of mind is even suspected of being a factor, investigators should consider using a Breathalyzer if the accused is willing to consent. In any event, voluntariness will be questioned whenever impairment or intoxication is involved.

SUMMARY

1. Threats made or significant inducements offered by persons in authority will render a confession inadmissible.

2. Trickery, deception, or prolonged interrogation may also invalidate a confession.

3. The state of mind of the accused is important in determining whether his or her statement was truly voluntary.

KEY TERMS

confession

person in authority

inducements

privilege against self-incrimination

REVIEW

■ TRUE OR FALSE?

_____ 1. The police may question the accused before he or she is informed of the right to counsel.

_____ 2. A victim may be considered the agent of a person in authority.

_____ 3. Threatening violence is an example of an inducement, whereas offering a lighter sentence is not.

_____ 4. The burden of proving that a statement is voluntary is on the prosecution.

_____ 5. The defence may introduce an accused's statement to show prior inconsistency.

_____ 6. If an accused is drunk at the time his or her statement is taken, the statement may later be found to have been involuntary.

_____ 7. To get an accused to confess, it is acceptable to make him or her believe that his or her co-accused has confessed.

■ MULTIPLE CHOICE

1. For the purpose of proving voluntariness, a "person in authority" or agent of that person may include

   a. the parents of the suspect

   b. a member of the clergy

   c. the victim of the crime

   d. any of the above

2. It is believed that involuntary statements should be inadmissible for the following reason:

   a. the courts should not ally themselves with the improper conduct of the investigators

   b. coerced evidence is often true

   c. officers need to be taught that coercion is inappropriate

   d. none of the above

■ FILL IN THE BLANKS

1. A confession is admissible only if it is proved _____ to have been voluntary.

2. An investigator must not offer _____ when interviewing an accused.

3. Prolonged interrogation may be considered coercive and result in an accused's statement being _____ from the trial.

4. The accused's state of mind may be called into question if the accused is in shock or is _____.

■ SHORT ANSWER

1. Give three examples of conduct by an officer that might amount to offering an inducement.

2. If an accused is impaired and is charged with a major crime, what should the investigator do before asking the accused to make a statement?

3. Why must investigators, when questioning an accused, be careful in making reference to the statements/confession of a co-accused?

CHAPTER 9
Disclosure Obligations

CHAPTER OBJECTIVES

After completing this chapter, you should be able to:

◆ Define the prosecution's disclosure obligations.

◆ Explain why the prosecution but not the defence must disclose.

◆ Explain how the defence may access records held by third parties.

DISCLOSURE

The Crown must **disclose** to the defence all relevant material regarding its case against the accused, whether or not the material is inculpatory (supportive of guilt) or exculpatory (supportive of innocence) and whether or not the Crown intends to introduce it at trial. This entails a lot of photocopying. The defence needs all of this material—witness statements, police officers' notes, and so on—to see exactly what evidence the Crown has against the accused—that is, the defence needs to judge the **case to meet**. This has a great impact on defence strategy: if the defence sees that the Crown has a very weak and circumstantial case, at the end of the Crown's case defence counsel may simply stand up and request a dismissal on the basis that the Crown has not made a case proving the accused guilty beyond a reasonable doubt. The defence will argue that the judge must therefore dismiss the charges.

The defence has no reciprocal obligation to disclose evidence to the Crown. After the Crown has presented its case, the defence, for the most part, is entitled to surprise the Crown with its defence. Consider, for example, a case where Greg is charged with assaulting Martha. The Crown attempts to prove all the elements of the offence of assault (s. 265(1) of the *Criminal Code*). It succeeds in proving that Greg intentionally applied force to Martha. That is the end of the Crown's case. At that point, the defence lawyer stands up and, without the Crown knowing what he is about to say, claims that Greg was acting in self-defence and that Martha was the aggressor. Additionally, the defence produces a witness who testifies to having seen the entire incident.

The defence is entitled to surprise the Crown in this manner, but such a turn of events is unlikely because the Crown and the defence usually attempt to resolve issues before going to trial. The defence is entitled

disclosure
a duty to show one's own evidence to the opposing party in a case

case to meet
usually, the sum of the prosecution's evidence (which dictates the evidence necessary to mount a supportable defence)

to surprise the Crown, but not vice versa, because the purpose of a criminal prosecution is not to obtain a conviction at any cost but to give the court what the Crown considers is credible evidence pertaining to the alleged crime. Crown counsel have a duty to see that all the available legal proof of the facts is presented, and the Crown should present its arguments both firmly and fairly to establish the evidence's legitimate strengths. The role of the prosecutor should not include any notion of winning or losing, and the entire prosecutorial team, including police officers, should be on their guard against this notion, for a criminal conviction is a very serious blight on a person's life. The Crown should treat its work as an exercise of public duty, and perform its functions efficiently and with integrity and fairness.

Full and frank disclosure is also important because it may help to bring about the early resolution of a case. For example, once an accused and his or her counsel realize how strong a case the Crown has, they may decide to plead guilty and avoid a long trial.

All relevant evidence needs to be disclosed. The material need not be credible or even capable of becoming evidence, but when in doubt about whether a piece of evidence is relevant, it is safer to err on the side of disclosure. Initial disclosure should occur before the accused is called on to plead (guilty or innocent), but there is a continuing obligation to disclose when additional material becomes available. In some circumstances the Crown has some discretion to withhold or delay disclosure, for example to protect the identity of informers, but the disclosure issue may ultimately be decided by the trial judge.

There are some items that should not be disclosed at all, or should be subject to delayed disclosure. The following are disclosure guidelines for Crown counsel (Royal Canadian Mounted Police, 1998):

1. Irrelevant information should not be disclosed.

2. Privileged information (including identity of informants).

3. Information protected by Statute (*Canada Evidence Act*, Federal *Privacy Act*).

4. Information that would reveal confidential police investigative techniques.

5. The existence and identity of those who will NOT be called to testify. For example: tipsters and persons assured anonymity through programs such as Crimestoppers.

6. Copies of police notes where all the relevant information has been provided elsewhere (in reports to Crown counsel). Any copies of police notebooks that must be disclosed are to be edited to remove information as noted above (usually just names and addresses—inked out in black ink and then re-photocopied).

7. Internal memos or notes dealing with legal opinions, advice etc. However, communication between a police officer and a Crown Counsel may be deemed to be unprotected and subject to disclosure.

8. Information not in possession of the Crown Counsel or investigating agency e.g. Ministry of Social Services (Defence can obtain on their own).

9. DELAY disclosure where:

   i. witness is at risk. To prevent harassment or injury, the identity and location of the person shall not be disclosed until the person testifies, or is no longer at risk.

   ii. an investigation is ongoing and disclosure of information would jeopardize the results. Relevant information should be withheld until the investigation is complete.

10. RESTRICT disclosure where:

   i. video tapes dealing with sexual assault are involved. Reasonable opportunity to view should be allowed, but defence counsel should not be provided with a copy of the tape.

The Crown is not obligated to disclose items in the possession of third parties. However, should the Crown acquire these records, they must be disclosed to the defence. An example of a third-party record of interest to the defence would be notes made by a rape crisis centre counsellor in a case where the victim may have given information to the counsellor about the suspected rapist. Other examples include hospital, psychiatric, and other kinds of victim-counselling records. The defence may believe that these records go toward proving that the victim is less worthy of being believed because he or she has a mental condition. Usually, Crown counsel avoid trying to access these records because they realize that the records will have to be disclosed to defence counsel once they are in the Crown's possession. Crown counsel do not wish to frustrate the defence, but often believe that such records will simply embarrass the victim and violate his or her privacy without providing any probative information.

If defence counsel are determined to access these records, they must do so in court before a judge. The procedure is set out in s. 278.2 of the *Criminal Code*:

1. First, the accused must demonstrate the likely relevance of the records—in other words, the reasonable possibility that information which is logically probative to an issue at trial, including the credibility or believability of the complainant, will be revealed in the records.

2. If the judge is satisfied that the likely relevance criterion has been met, the third-party counsellor must hand over the **counselling records** to the judge. The judge must then read the materials and decide whether they are relevant. Assuming that the records are relevant to some extent, the judge must also balance the victim's privacy against the accused's right to make a full answer and defence. At this point the judge may decide not to disclose the records, or to disclose them only in part.

   counselling records
   notes and records made in the course of providing counselling services to a client/patient

3. After the defence has gained access to some or all of the records, the records still will not be admissible unless it can convince the court, by demonstrating their probative value, that they are necessary to the defence.

Section 278.5(2) of the *Criminal Code* sets out the factors that the judge should consider in determining whether to order the production of the records for review. It states:

> the judge shall consider the salutary and deleterious effects of the determination on the accused's right to make a full answer and defence and on the right to privacy and equality of the complainant or witness, as the case may be, and any other person to whom the record relates. In particular, the judge shall take the following factors into account:
>
> (a) the extent to which the record is necessary for the accused to make a full answer and defence;
>
> (b) the probative value of the record;
>
> (c) the nature and extent of the reasonable expectation of privacy with respect to the record;
>
> (d) whether production of the record is based on a discriminatory belief or bias;
>
> (e) the potential prejudice to the personal dignity and right to privacy of any person to whom the record relates;
>
> (f) society's interest in encouraging the reporting of sexual offences;
>
> (g) society's interest in encouraging the obtaining of treatment by complainants of sexual offences; and
>
> (h) the effect of the determination on the integrity of the trial process.

SUMMARY

1. The Crown must disclose all relevant material to the defence.

2. The defence needs this information so that it can know the case to meet.

3. The Crown need not disclose irrelevant information, privileged information, internal memos, or information not in its possession.

4. The defence may apply to the judge to gain access to third-party records, but it must demonstrate likely relevance before the judge will examine the records.

KEY TERMS

disclosure   counselling records

case to meet

REVIEW

∎ TRUE OR FALSE?

_____   1.   The advantage of surprise is all on the side of the defence.

_____   2.   The goal of the Crown is to convict the guilty.

_____   3.   Privileged information must be disclosed to the defence.

_____   4.   The names of tipsters need not be disclosed.

_____   5.   If the defence requires the accused's counselling records, the Crown must obtain them from the third party.

∎ MULTIPLE CHOICE

1.   Rape crisis centre records may be accessed by the defence if it can prove

   a.   likely relevance

   b.   necessity and reliability

   c.   prior inconsistency

   d.   recent complaint

2.   If the Crown has already fulfilled its disclosure obligations, but then receives a new piece of exculpatory evidence, it

   a.   may decide to keep the evidence to itself

   b.   may return the evidence to the source (if the Crown does not have the evidence, the defence cannot have it)

   c.   must disclose it to the defence (disclosure obligations are ongoing)

   d.   none of the above

∎ FILL IN THE BLANKS

1.   The defence does not have to give the Crown any of its material, for it has no _____.

2.   The Crown may not have to disclose the identity of

   _____.

3.   When the judge looks over third-party counselling records, he or she is considering the _____ of the accused's right to make full answer and defence versus the victim's right to privacy.

■ SHORT ANSWER

1. Name three types of evidence that the Crown does not have to disclose.

2. Explain why the defence has no reciprocal obligation of disclosure.

3. Formulate an argument in support of the position that defence counsel should not have access to a rape crisis centre's counselling records on the victim in a sexual assault trial.

CHAPTER 10
Evidence Skills for Police

CHAPTER OBJECTIVES

After completing this chapter, you should be able to:

◆ Understand how to take proper notes that will hold up in court.

◆ Understand how to testify in chief.

◆ Understand how to overcome the rigours of cross-examination.

TAKING NOTES THAT WILL HOLD UP IN COURT

It is very important that officers take accurate and timely **duty notes**, because many people will be counting on the notes' accuracy during a case. Crown counsel will rely on the notes to reconstruct the time-frame of and events surrounding the offence. Defence counsel will attempt to prove that the notes are inaccurate. The Crown, defence, and judge will all need photocopies of the notes.

Officers will often refer to their notebooks to refresh their memory when testifying. If an officer refers to his or her notebook during examination-in-chief, the opposing counsel are entitled to see the notebook before commencing cross-examination. Before any use can be made of the notes, however, the officer must obtain permission from the judge. A good way to ask is, Your Honour, may I refresh my memory by referring to my notes? Permission is often prefaced by a few questions concerning whether the notes were made around the same time as the events they record. The judge may ask, for example,

◆ When did you make the notes?

◆ Did you make the notes from memory or did you consult with other officers before making the notes?

◆ Were the events fresh in your mind when you made the notes?

◆ Where were you when you made the notes?

◆ Have you made any additions or deletions since you first made the notes?

The judge may also ask whether the officer has any **independent recollection** of the events in question—in other words, whether the officer is able to remember the events to which he or she is testifying or is

duty notes
an officer's written record of the details of his or her attendance at a crime scene, an arrest, or a field investigation

independent recollection
a recollection of events being recounted in testimony that is separate from what can be gleaned from reading one's notes about those events

simply repeating what is in the notes. This may affect how much weight the officer's testimony is given.

When defence counsel examine the officer's notebook, they will be looking for

1. use of the same pen throughout the relevant entry,

2. spacing consistent with other notes in the notebook, and

3. a style of note taking consistent with other notes in the notebook (with regard to accuracy, use of abbreviations, method of noting names, dates, and addresses, and level of vocabulary and grammar).

Defence counsel will be on the lookout for a police witness's description of an event that uses words the same as those in another officer's notebook. Counsel will attempt to insinuate that the officer attempted to ensure that his or her notes would corroborate what the other officer wrote. Such collaboration between officers, formerly very common, is extremely ill-advised. It implies that the officer recorded not what actually happened but what the other officers wanted him or her to record—in short, it suggests a lack of truthfulness. Hence, officers should always prepare their notes on their own and in their own style. They should ensure that the notes are consistently spaced and dated, and that only one writing instrument is used on each occasion.

SUMMARY

1. Officers must ask permission before using their notes in court.

2. Defence counsel will have an opportunity to examine officers' notes.

3. Officers must never collaborate with each other when they are making notes on a particular incident.

TIPS FOR GIVING TESTIMONY

Officers are asked to testify for many reasons, for example, to provide eyewitness testimony, to demonstrate continuity of evidence, or on a *voir dire* to establish the voluntariness of a confession. It is important to remember several things when testifying:

1. Speak loudly and clearly, making sure that you say yes or no instead of nodding or shaking your head, for the court reporter must be able to record a vocal response.

2. Speak directly to the person who is asking the question.

3. Be respectful of the court and address a justice of the peace as "Your Worship" and a judge as "Your Honour."

4. Ask permission before referring to your notes. The justice or judge or may wish to question you about how contemporaneous the notes are before allowing their use in court.

5. Expect interruptions from defence counsel. Often, defence counsel will stand up and say "Objection!" when the Crown is attempting to ask the officer key questions during the examination-in-chief. You must stop speaking when the defence lawyer begins to speak, and resume only when the judge says it is all right to do so. Try to make sure that your testimony is as free of hearsay, irrelevant or privileged information, and opinion as possible—defence counsel will have fewer reasons to interrupt you.

6. It is easy to become disconcerted during cross-examination and by interruptions from defence counsel on examination-in-chief, and it is difficult not to take counsel's comments as a personal affront. It is a good idea to try to remain as impartial as possible and not to reveal your feelings about events or individuals.

Officers are frequently asked to testify as eyewitnesses. Consider the example of a vice team or unit gathering evidence on the activities of an escort agency. Often an officer or two will be asked to go undercover and pose as escorts looking for work. They may obtain information from the owners or managers on how the business is run, and thus become eyewitnesses to the offence of living off the avails of prostitution (ss. 212(i) and 212(j) of the *Criminal Code*).

The eyewitness testimony of officers will be challenged in particular ways by defence counsel. It is a good idea to prepare for these challenges, because knowing what to expect can give you greater confidence in facing the rigours of cross-examination.

Beware of leading questions! Defence counsel will use leading questions during cross-examination to get an officer to agree to a skewed set of facts or circumstances, and thereby attempt to make the officer look less credible. Defence counsel will question

1. *Location*   Defence counsel will argue that the officer could not possibly have been in a position to make observations as accurate as the ones claimed. Consider, for example, an officer who (without trespassing on private property) conducted a **perimeter search** of the backyard of a house belonging to a person suspected of growing marijuana. The officer claims that he could see the marijuana simply by looking into the backyard. Defence counsel will argue that certain impediments—shrubbery, a lamppost, poor lighting, and the presence of azaleas (which have leaves similar to those of marijuana)—would have made it impossible to observe the marijuana from such a vantage point.

    perimeter search
    usually, a search that consists of observations of a piece of private property made without physical intrusion on that property

2. *State of mind*   Defence counsel will further argue that the witness's observations were influenced by the witness's beliefs and state of mind. Counsel will argue, for example, that because the officer

expected to find marijuana, his or her expectations coloured his or her observations of the backyard.

3. *Memory*   Defence counsel will attempt to argue that the passage of time since the events in question has hampered the witness's ability to recall what occurred.

4. *Truthfulness*   Defence counsel, without intending a personal affront, will suggest that an officer is lying. Counsel will insinuate that because the officer disliked or zealously wished to convict their client, the officer was prejudiced against their client and motivated to lie in order to secure inculpatory evidence.

This is all part of the game of cross-examination, which supposedly is a safeguard against false testimony, and such allegations are thus par for the course. By anticipating such questions, maintaining a commitment to tell the truth, and keeping a calm demeanour, a police witness will be able to remain credible under the scrutiny of cross-examination.

SUMMARY

1. Address the court loudly, clearly, and respectfully.

2. Expect interruptions and objections from defence counsel.

3. Remain impartial and do not let defence counsel intimidate you.

4. As an eyewitness, you must be ready for challenges to your state of mind (the issue of suggestibility), memory, truthfulness, and ability to observe the events in question from your claimed location.

KEY TERMS

duty notes   perimeter search

independent recollection

REVIEW

■ TRUE OR FALSE?

_____   **1.** Collaborating with other officers when making notes is an acceptable practice.

_____   **2.** An officer must request permission from the judge before using his or her notes in court.

_____   **3.** Nodding and shaking of the head are acceptable and clearly understood means of communication in court.

■ FILL IN THE BLANKS

1. In court, a justice of the peace is referred to as Your
   _____.

2. If you can remember an incident, and are not simply reading your
   notes, you have an _____ of that incident.

3. Defence counsel will attempt to make a witness agree to a different
   set of facts by using _____ questions.

■ SHORT ANSWER

1. Imagine a situation where an officer will be asked to testify as an
   eyewitness.

2. Pretend to be defence counsel and pick holes in the observations
   that would be made by the officer in question 1.

PART II

An Introduction to Forensic Science and the Collection of Physical Evidence

CHAPTER 11

The Preservation, Collection, and Continuity of Physical Evidence

CHAPTER OBJECTIVES

After completing this chapter, you should be able to:

◆ Describe how a crime scene should be secured.

◆ Describe how potentially dangerous materials at a crime scene should be handled.

◆ Explain the term "continuity of possession" and describe how continuity is maintained.

INTRODUCTION

Physical evidence is any material or substance, no matter how small, that proves or assists in proving any element of a criminal charge, including the identity of the victim or perpetrator. Physical evidence may be used to strengthen and corroborate the testimony of witnesses or to disprove statements made by an accused. The police investigator may use physical evidence in the discovery and identification of suspects.

The acquisition and handling of physical evidence is paramount to the success of criminal investigations. Conclusions drawn by investigators may be erroneous if the evidence on which these conclusions are based has been contaminated. Contaminated evidence is of little or no value to the investigator. This chapter examines the proper collection and preservation of evidence and the significance of the evidence in and of itself.

Included in the acquisition of physical evidence is the requirement to mark the evidence in a prescribed manner to ensure continuity of possession. The continuity aspect of evidence will be discussed in this chapter, as will be the likely results of a police officer's failure to maintain continuity.

THE PRESERVATION OF EVIDENCE AND THE CRIME SCENE

crime scene
the location where a crime has been or is suspected to have been committed

The **crime scene** is generally regarded as the best or primary source of physical evidence. The residence of a suspect or a place at which the crime occurred is an excellent secondary source for physical evidence. Physical evidence found at a crime scene may identify a suspect as having been at the scene or in contact with someone or something at the scene. The importance of securing and preserving the scene cannot be overemphasized. Evidence lost because a crime scene remained unsecured can never be recovered.

The preservation of the crime scene is the responsibility of the first officer on the scene. If this were the only duty of the first officer, the task would be daunting enough; however, the first officer is responsible for a number of other tasks. In addition to handling emergencies he or she may encounter on arrival, and looking after witnesses and victims, the first officer must be mindful of the potential for contamination and destruction of the crime scene. The multiple duties of the first officer demand a clear and alert mind and an individual with the knowledge necessary to carry out his or her responsibilities.

On his or her arrival at the crime scene, the first officer must of course take action to ensure that the situation he or she encounters does not deteriorate. Preventing loss of life or injury is the foremost concern; this, of course, may include the arrest of a suspect who is still on the scene.

The first officer on the scene is the person responsible for preserving the scene in as nearly an undisturbed condition as possible. After attending to the most pressing duties (arresting suspects, assisting the injured, and eliminating potential risks generally), the first officer must decide what the crime scene's boundaries are. The crime scene generally consists

crime scene core
the immediate location of the crime

crime scene perimeter
the area surrounding the crime scene core and including potential routes to and from the core

of a **core** and a **perimeter**. The core is the area in which the criminal action took place; the perimeter is the area surrounding the core that contains the likely entry and exit paths taken by the suspect or suspects. Once the boundaries have been determined, the first officer must take steps to protect the area.

securing the crime scene
a group of tasks that must be carried out by an officer arriving at a crime scene, including protecting from disturbance any potential evidence, and controlling access by other parties

Foremost in the thoughts of the first officer on the scene is the task of **securing the crime scene** in such a manner as to prevent accidental or intentional contamination by anyone at or near the scene, including police officers and other official personnel. The first officer should determine the best route to and through the crime scene for those who have work to do at the scene. The route chosen by the first officer should be one that, when used by others, will disturb as little potential evidence as possible. An indication of the route chosen by the first officer should be included in his or her notes. The route will also be indicated on the schematic of the crime scene that the officer or another member of the force will prepare.

The first officer at the scene should position himself or herself, or another officer, so as to deter access to the scene and observe anyone who enters the scene. Notations in the officer's notebook should include the name and rank or position of anyone entering and leaving the scene, and include times of arrival and departure. Police and other personnel having duties to perform at the scene may include ambulance and fire personnel, the forensic team, the criminal investigations officer, and the coroner. At no time should members of the public (including property owners, the victim's family and friends, and the media) be admitted to the scene.

The first officer and others at the scene must be alert to the potential for inadvertent contamination of the scene. An officer who puts down a hat or other article of clothing within the bounds of the crime scene may introduce material that will invalidate finds made at the scene. Police use of a telephone that is part of the scene may eliminate the record of the last call made to that telephone. Flushing a toilet, using a sink, smoking, and turning lights or appliances on or off are all acts that can disturb a crime scene. Most of the acts that can lead to contamination or destruction of evidence at a crime scene can be avoided, however, by using common sense. Unless an aspect of the scene poses a threat to human life, that aspect should not be altered. If the crime scene is a mess, it should remain a mess until the examination of the scene by the police and other personnel is completed.

Police officers have the authority to cordon off and refuse entry to a crime scene under s. 129(a) of the *Criminal Code*. Although it does not specifically address crime scene security, s. 129(a) does provide for the arrest and punishment for any person obstructing a police officer in the lawful execution of his or her duties. What constitutes the lawful execution of a police officer's duties has been determined by case law. *R v. Knowlton* (1973) states that a police officer is lawfully executing his or her duties when he or she refuses admittance to anyone attempting to enter an area cordoned off by police. The police therefore have the legal authority to cordon off and protect the crime scene.

The determination of when a crime scene may be released—that is, removed from police control—is made by the officer in charge of the investigation, unless the investigation involves a death, in which case the security of the scene is under the coroner's authority (as set forth in the *Coroner's Act* of Ontario). This Act allows police and others acting under their control to seize anything relevant to the investigation at the crime scene and to maintain the security of the scene until the scene is ordered released by the coroner (usually following the **post mortem examination**).

post mortem examination
an examination of a dead body made to determine such issues as the cause and time of death; an autopsy

SECURITY AND CONTINUITY OF POSSESSION

Some forms of physical evidence (such as a weapon at the scene of a homicide or assault) are readily identifiable as evidence, while other evidence (such as fingerprints) requires detection, collection, and interpretation by experts (such as members of a mobile crime lab or **identification officers**). Whether a crime scene should be examined by experts depends to a large degree on the severity of the crime. It is unreasonable to expect

identification officer
police officer with special training in the analysis of physical evidence

that a crime involving minimal damage to property or small-scale theft will warrant expert attention. On the other hand, investigations in situations involving loss of life, extensive physical injury, or serious crimes against persons or property (such as sexual assault, robbery, and kidnapping) usually warrant the use of experts. But whether experts are involved or not, it is still incumbent on the investigating officer to protect, collect, mark for identification, and maintain the continuity of all crime scene evidence.

When evidence is located at a crime scene or anywhere else, its location should be noted in the discovering officer's notebook. A description of the evidence and a note on the time of discovery should also be included. Whenever possible, there should be a photograph of the evidence, taken in place. When including a photograph is not possible, the location of the evidence should be noted on a schematic diagram of the crime scene or other location.

Most police departments equip their patrol cars or officers with evidence collection kits. These kits can include disposable cameras, tape measures, graph paper, rubber or latex gloves, surgical protective masks, plastic bags of various sizes, adhesive labels or tags, and bottles, vials and other containers or materials for packing evidence. A novice police officer should know how to properly use these items for collecting, marking, and preserving evidence.

The Ontario Forensic Science Laboratory, located in Toronto, makes available to all police officers in the province a manual that provides precise instructions on the handling and packaging of materials sent to the laboratory for examination. The Royal Canadian Mounted Police publish a similar manual, which is available to that force's members. These manuals describe methods for packing evidence such as accelerants in arson cases, blood samples, fibres, soil, and hair. An abridged version of the RCMP forensic manual is reproduced in the appendix.

Contaminated Materials

The transmission of infectious diseases through the handling of contaminated materials is a major concern for police officers. The increased possibility of contact with such contaminated material in today's society has caused police departments to take steps to minimize the possibility of harm to their officers. The ease with which HIV (AIDS), hepatitis B, and other potentially lethal diseases can be transmitted demands that precautions be taken by those who risk exposure.

The wearing of latex, rubber, or puncture-proof Kevlar gloves may be called for in situations involving the collection of evidence related to intravenous drug use or assaults on and homicides of persons suspected of being infected with HIV. Police officers should be aware of the potential for exposure at a variety of crime scenes, including the danger of reaching into the pockets of drug suspects during a body search, for inserting an unprotected hand into a pocket or other spot hidden from view during a drug search may have deadly consequences. Police officers should learn how to recognize signs of intravenous drug use that can be encountered during a search.

Evidence that is or that may be contaminated must be handled and packed in a way that reduces or eliminates the risk to others who may be required to handle or examine such evidence. Evidence suspected of contamination must be sealed in a clear plastic exhibit bag and marked in a way that conspicuously indicates its suspected contamination. This evidence should not be forwarded to a crime lab or other agency until instructions have been received from that agency concerning the procedure involved in transporting the evidence.

Continuity of Possession

Crime scene evidence that is relevant to a case will eventually be introduced in court. The admissibility of this evidence is determined by, among other things, the rules concerning continuity of possession. Continuity of possession is often misunderstood to mean the continuous physical possession of evidence in one person's hands from its time of seizure to its appearance in court. Establishing continuity of possession is possible, however, even when the evidence passes into other hands, though the police officer introducing the evidence in court must still account for its whereabouts from its time of seizure to its appearance in court. To preserve continuity, this accounting must include a record of any person or persons who may have had contact with the evidence. It is naive to believe that a police officer who seizes an item will have it in his or her physical possession until it is called for in court. Evidence can vary in size from a minute particle to the contents of a building, thus making physical possession impossible in many cases.

Most police departments give their officers lockers for maintaining evidence for brief periods (the time allowed varies from department to department). Evidence seized by an officer must eventually be bagged and tagged for placement in designated evidence storage facilities. **Exhibit reports** completed by the officer who seized the evidence or the officer assigned to maintain the evidence should accompany the evidence. Any change in custody of evidence should be noted in the file by the case officer to facilitate location of that evidence for court purposes. Movement from the exhibit or property storage should be noted in the case file to allow for accountability by the officer introducing the evidence in court.

Samples of drug evidence often need to be moved temporarily to a laboratory for analysis during the storage period. The quantity removed for analysis should be noted, as well as the date, the time, and the name of the officer handling the removal. The date and time should be recorded in the officer's notebook, as should an account of what was done with the sample. The identity of anyone removing a piece of evidence from a storage facility should be noted by the storage facility custodian, whose notes must also include the date and time the evidence was removed. This applies to all evidence, and to instances where a piece of evidence is simply examined rather than removed.

exhibit report
a standard form document that accompanies a piece of physical evidence and provides a description of the item and a record of any changes in its custody (such as out to a pathology lab and back) prior to trial

Known Standards or Standards for Comparison

There are two reasons for sending potential evidence to a crime lab. First, scientific examination of material submitted to a lab is conducted to determine its composition and origin. Scientific examination of narcotics can reveal the specific narcotic in a sample. A qualitative and quantitative examination will further indicate the purity of the sample—that is, what proportion of the sample contains the narcotic in question.

EXAMPLE   Sample received from Sgt. James Black of the Metropolitan Toronto Police Department on the 5th of June 1998 at 09:00 hrs. Examination of the off-white powder-like material indicates that the sample (weight: 10 grams) is 85 percent cocaine hydrochloride. The balance of the sample (15 percent) is milk sugar.

**known standards/
standards for comparison**
*samples of evidence (of the same
type) collected or prepared for
the purpose of analytical
comparison with the evidence to
be used at trial; control samples*

Second, in addition to being asked to conduct a qualitative and quantitative analysis of the evidence, lab personnel are often asked to determine the point of origin of an item and whether that item was originally part of a larger quantity of the same material. To answer these questions, **known standards** or **samples for comparison** are often required. A known standards sample must be handled, stored, and transported in the same way and with the same diligence as other evidence. Evidence and comparison samples should always be packed separately to ensure accurate test results. In a case where burnt matches are found at a crime scene and a suspect is found to have paper matches in his or her pocket on arrest, both sets of matches should be handled in precisely the same manner. Both sets will be shipped to the lab for comparison, but each set should be packed and sealed separately. The same procedure applies when comparing soil found on a suspect's shoes and soil at a crime scene.

The results of a test involving comparisons to known standards may be sufficient to indicate that a suspect was present at a crime scene, may have been present, or was not present at all. Test results may further indicate that a suspect was in contact with the victim (as indicated, for example, by the presence of a victim's blood on the clothing or person of the suspect).

Marking and Identification of Evidence

Evidence must be marked to facilitate its identification in court. Police officers most often mark a piece of physical evidence for identification by scratching the officer's initials or name on the object or, where possible, by writing the officer's name in ink on the object. Some evidence, however, is impossible to mark in this manner. Trace evidence, microscopic evidence, and any evidence that is too fragile for physical contact requires other means of identification. In the case of **latent evidence** (evidence that requires collection using chemical reagents or other scientific means), hair, or fibres, the item's location should be noted by the technician or officer seizing the evidence. A thorough description of any evi-

latent evidence
*evidence that must be collected
or interpreted with the
assistance of special technology,
such as the application of a
chemical reagent*

dence unsuitable for marking must be included in the notes of the officer who seizes the evidence.

On occasion, officers seize evidence that is impractical to bring to court (vehicles, windows, furniture, blood stains on a floor or on the seats of a vehicle, and so forth). In cases where bringing an original item into court (as called for by the "best evidence rule") is impractical, the rule allows photographs to be substituted. The definition of photographs includes still photographs, motion pictures, and videotape. On rare occasions a judge may, as provided for in s. 652 of the *Criminal Code*, allow a jury to leave the courtroom to visit a site at which evidence was located. In cases where photographs are brought to court in lieu of original evidence, the person who took the photographs must be present to introduce them into evidence. Under certain conditions, however, s. 491.2(3) of the *Criminal Code* allows photographs to be entered into evidence without the photographer's attendance in court if they are accompanied by an affidavit sworn by the photographer. It should also be noted that s. 491.2(4) allows the evidence of a police officer who has seized evidence to be admitted into court via a solemn declaration in lieu of the officer's attendance in court. These sections of the Code were put in place to expedite the trial.

Schematic Diagrams and Photographs

More serious investigations, particularly those relating to incidents where injuries occurred, may require photographs or schematic diagrams of the crime scene. In larger police departments, producing these records is the responsibility of a forensic investigation or identification team; in smaller departments the first officer or the investigating officer may be required to complete the task.

As is sometimes the case, an enlarged schematic diagram (drawn to scale) will be used in court to demonstrate where evidence was located. The purpose of the schematic diagram is to provide accurate measurements of objects at the crime scene and indicate their proximity to one another. This helps witnesses clarify their testimony regarding the crime scene. It should be noted that schematic diagrams indicate *position*, whereas photographs demonstrate *condition*.

The schematic diagram of a crime scene must clearly indicate its scale. North should always be at the top of the page. A compass drawing indicating the four cardinal points should be included, as should a legend identifying objects in the diagram. Measurements and other notations on the drawing should be easily readable and the result of careful efforts by trained personnel.

Departmental Directives on Evidence

Most police departments—particularly the large metropolitan forces, the Ontario Provincial Police, and the Royal Canadian Mounted Police—have policies that spell out the procedures for the seizure, handling, and storage of evidence. Procedures may vary slightly from department to department, but all procedures are designed to safeguard the continuity of evidence. The following is a distillation of the procedures followed by most police departments.

A police officer who locates potential evidence during an investigation or search shall indicate and note its location by making appropriate measurements from fixed points at the scene. The object's or item's location, together with the time and date of discovery, shall be noted in the officer's notebook.

When present at the crime scene, the officer in charge of the investigation (case officer) shall be advised of the discovery of said evidence.

When applicable, the item located should be photographed in place by an identification officer or an officer assigned to this duty.

The item seized should be handled in a manner consistent with instructions on the preservation and packaging of specific items published by the Ontario Forensic Science Laboratory. Evidence seized for comparison shall be packaged and handled separately to avoid the possibility of contamination.

Where appropriate and possible, the officer seizing the evidence shall mark such evidence by placing his or her initials, together with the date and time of seizure, on the item itself. Where a direct marking of the exhibit is impractical, the officer shall place the item in an appropriate designated container and complete the prescribed tag or label attached to the container (exhibit bag, box, or plastic container).

No exhibit shall be left unattended from its time of seizure until the item can be deposited in the police property storage facility.

On returning to the office, the officer seizing the item, or the case officer, shall secure the evidence directly in the police property locker in conjunction with the duty property clerk.

The transfer of any evidence required to be examined by the forensic lab shall be the responsibility of the case officer and/or his or her designate.

The transfer of evidence to and from court remains the responsibility of the case officer. No exhibit shall be removed from the control of the property clerk without appropriate authority and signatures.

THE INTRODUCTION OF EVIDENCE INTO COURT

The following hypothetical examination of a police officer by Crown counsel illustrates how evidence is introduced into court.

Q. Officer, were you present at 226 Lakeshore Drive, Burlington, Ontario on the 6th of May 1998?

A. Yes I was.

Q. What activities, if any, did you take part in while at that location?

A. I was part of a three-member team of Halton Regional Police officers assigned to search the residence at that location for evidence relevant to the assault on Mrs. Irma LaChance.

Q. What, if anything, did you find during that search?

A. At approximately 13:30 hours on that date I found a black-handled knife with a six-inch blade. I found the knife on the floor in the kitchen area of the house. The knife was in front of the kick-plate of the kitchen cabinets, approximately four feet from a hot air register and approximately eight inches away from the kick-plate.

Q. Can you point to this location on the enlarged schematic diagram?

A. It was approximately here, where the "X" is located. I made note of its location in my notebook immediately upon discovering the knife.

Q. What, if anything, did you do with the knife upon discovery?

A. Using a pair of wooden tongs provided in the evidence kit I carry, I picked the knife up by placing the tongs on the hilt or guard of the knife. I used my penknife to place my initials on the top of the handle portion of the knife. Included with my initials was the date 06-05-98. I then placed the knife into a plastic evidence bag, again provided in my collection kit. I then sealed the bag and filled in the label portion of the exhibit bag. This included my name, rank, department, the time and date the object was located, and a brief description of the evidence found.

Q. What else, if anything, did you do?

A. I advised Detective Sergeant Robertson of my finds and entered the details of that conversation in my notebook. I then placed the knife in my briefcase and transported it to the police department headquarters. I then took the knife in the sealed exhibit bag and turned it over directly to Constable Edwards, the HQ property clerk. In my presence, Constable Edwards filled out the exhibit report, including the date and time I delivered the exhibit. I then signed the report and took a copy of that exhibit report.

Q. Officer, do you have a key to the property room and have you had any contact with that exhibit since turning it over to the property clerk?

A. I do not have a key nor access of any kind to the property vault, and I have not seen the exhibit since I turned it over to Constable Edwards.

Q. Officer, I now show you a plastic bag containing what appears to be a black-handled knife with a six-inch blade, marked "B" for identification. What, if anything, can you tell me about this object?

A. The plastic bag label is in my handwriting and contains the information I placed on the label on the date and at the time indicated. The knife inside the bag is the knife I found at the scene, as indicated in my earlier testimony, and I know this to be true because my initials and the date are clearly visible at the top of the handle.

Q. Does that conclude your testimony on your actions relevant to this investigation?

A. It does.

While the above example of an officer's testimony may appear routine, it is routine only because the officer took the time to follow proper procedures for the acquisition and storage of evidence. Care taken during the course of an investigation, particularly in the handling of evidence, will likely result in an uncontested entry of that evidence into court. Following proper procedure ensures that one will be able to establish continuity of possession.

KEY TERMS

crime scene

crime scene core

crime scene perimeter

securing the crime scene

post mortem examination

identification officer

exhibit report

known standards/standards for comparison

latent evidence

REVIEW

■ SHORT ANSWER

1. Describe some of the consequences of conclusions based on contaminated evidence.

2. What constitutes the core and perimeter of a crime scene?

3. Who is responsible for establishing the best route for emergency personnel at a crime scene? What are some of the considerations to be taken into account in selecting this route?

4. What actions should the first officer take in protecting the crime scene?

5. Why should the police (first officer or other designated officer) note the names as well as the arrival and departure times of persons entering the crime scene?

6. Explain the term "continuity of possession" as it pertains to the introduction of evidence into court.

7. Why would thorough notes by a police officer help prove the continuity of a particular piece of evidence?

8. How is the case *R v. Knowlton* (1973) relevant to the protection of a crime scene?

9. Explain the term "known standards" as it applies to evidence sent to the forensic lab.

10. Describe an investigative crime scene where a police officer may encounter infected evidence.

11. This chapter notes several actions that could contaminate or destroy evidence if taken by a police officer attending a crime scene. Using your common sense, identify other kinds of actions by police or others at a crime scene that could contaminate or destroy evidence.

■ **CASE STUDY**

You are a police officer directed by the dispatcher to the scene of a break-and-enter and possible sexual assault. On arrival at the scene you notice that the front door of the house is open and damaged. You carefully enter and are met by a very distraught 25-year-old female who advises you that she awoke to find a masked male intruder in her house. She attempted to return to her bedroom and lock the door. However, she was intercepted by the intruder, who forced her to the floor at the entrance to her bedroom. The intruder then pulled a knife and told the victim that if she did not have sex with him he would kill her.

You report back to dispatch using your portable radio and request the attendance of Criminal Investigation Bureau (CIB) personnel and crime scene examiners. Just as you are about to secure the house as a crime scene area, the victim's husband arrives home. You meet him at the door, blocking his entrance, and tell him what has taken place. He insists on entering the house and speaking with his wife. He wants to call a doctor and insists that he be allowed to call his wife's sister on a telephone in the house.

While you are waiting for the CIB personnel and crime scene examiners, the victim advises you that she got a glimpse of her assailant's face as he left the house and removed the ski mask. She believes that she will be able to identify the assailant. She further advises that the assailant cut his hand on the door-frame as he was leaving. In addition, the victim advises that the assailant must have been in the house for some time, because she did not get out of bed for at least 10 minutes, thinking that the noise she heard at the front door was her husband returning home late from work. The victim advises that she was awakened by the noise at the front door at approximately 2:30 a.m. She checked the alarm clock at the bedside when she was awakened by the sound of breaking glass.

Using the information in this case study, answer the following questions:

1. What should you do about the husband's demand that he be allowed to see his wife?

2. What considerations should you take into account in defining the crime scene area and determining how you will protect that area?

3. What is the reason for creating a schematic diagram of the crime scene?

4. You begin to make a schematic diagram of the crime scene. What should be included in this drawing, and why?

5. What can photographs of a crime scene show that a schematic diagram cannot?

6. You wish to provide evidence of the damage done to the door-frame by the assailant on entering the premises. Removing the door-frame and bringing it to court does not seem feasible. Does the best evidence rule require producing the door-frame in court? Cite relevant law in your answer.

CHAPTER 12

Physical Evidence and Evidentiary Value

CHAPTER OBJECTIVES

After completing this chapter, you should be able to:

◆ Explain the evidentiary value of imprints and impressions.

◆ Describe the role of blood, semen, and urine testing in criminal investigations, and describe the advantages of DNA testing.

◆ Explain how forensic knowledge about firearms can assist criminal investigations.

INTRODUCTION

Finding physical evidence at or near a crime scene is of little value if the officers involved have no understanding of the significance of that evidence. This chapter will examine the characteristics of various forms of physical evidence and discuss what the physical evidence is likely to prove. Understanding the evidentiary value of physical evidence enables the investigator to draw accurate conclusions from that evidence. Recognizing the limitations of that physical evidence also gives the investigator the knowledge that his or her case may be incomplete.

Unlike eyewitness testimony, physical evidence does not change. Physical evidence has a higher evidentiary value than the testimony of witnesses and is therefore more reliable. The location of physical evidence left behind by the human body—fingerprints, blood, semen, and hair, for example—can place an accused at the scene of a crime. Some forms of physical evidence (fingerprints, DNA) are sufficient to establish a *prima facie* case, thereby placing the onus on the accused to refute the evidence or face conviction.

IMPRINTS AND IMPRESSIONS

When two objects come into contact, a **transference** of their properties onto each other occurs. However, evidence of such contact is not always detectable, for some materials lend themselves to transference more

transference
an imprint or trace left on one surface or object by another

147

readily than others. But as our scientific knowledge and abilities increase, so does our ability to detect and analyze contact.

Imprints and impressions are the markings left on a surface when two objects (one or both of which may be a person) come into contact. Impressions are made when a harder object comes into contact with a softer surface, as in the case of an impression made by a tool. Imprints are made when a softer object comes into contact with a harder surface, as in the case of a fingerprint. A tool's exterior characteristics will be visible as a reverse impression. For example, a crowbar used to pry open a door will leave a reverse impression on the softer wood of the door-frame. The impression will reflect not only the shape and other original characteristics of the tool, but also any marks made on the tool by prior use, such as scratches and chips.

The ability of a police forensic unit to successfully lift an imprint (such as a fingerprint) or, using the appropriate materials, to obtain an impression of the mark left by a tool, is key to the evidentiary value of the imprint or impression. The characteristics of the imprint or impression will be microscopically examined and, when compared with a known standard (the tool itself or a fingerprint taken from a suspect), indicate that the impression was made by the tool or the suspect's finger, as the case may be.

Most police officers would agree that of all the types of contact evidence, fingerprints have the highest evidentiary value. With the possible exception of DNA testing, fingerprints are the best way to identify a suspect and place him or her at the scene of a crime. Because fingerprints never change and are unique to each person, identifying a person by his or her fingerprints is virtually assured. Minor injuries do not alter the pattern of fingerprints, and scarring may in fact add to the uniqueness of a person's fingerprints.

All fingerprint patterns can be classified as one of three types: loops, whorls, and arches. Additional characteristics make a print unique to an individual. By comparing a print found at a crime scene with prints on file or newly taken from a suspect or accused, experts can tell whether the crime scene print was made by the person in question. The findings of fingerprint experts are seldom successfully challenged in court.

Some fingerprints are created when a suspect's or other person's fingers come into contact with an object (for example, glass, metal, a plastic bag, or wood) and a residue of oil and perspiration from the fingertips is deposited on the object's surface. This type of print is usually invisible to the eye and requires the application of chemicals or laser light to become

latent fingerprint
a fingerprint that is not easily observed by the naked eye and that must be collected through scientific means

visible. A print that is hidden from the eye is called a **latent** print. Fingerprints can be visible to the eye when they are the result of contact with a substance such as blood, dust, or grease previously deposited on a surface. For obvious reasons, these are called visible impressions. Fingerprints resulting from contact with a soft substance such as clay, wax, or putty are known as moulded prints because they leave a visible indentation in the substance.

Factors Affecting the Quality of Fingerprints

The quality and identifiability of prints depends on a number of factors. The size of the surface that makes contact with the fingers is one important factor. A larger surface area offers a better chance that a substantial portion of a finger will leave a print behind. Small items such as coins, nails, and the like are usually unsuitable for providing identifiable prints. The texture or makeup of a surface is a second factor that may affect the ability of an expert to expose a fingerprint. Smooth, non-porous surfaces are far more likely than irregular surfaces to produce good results. How much time has passed since the prints were made is another factor affecting the quality of prints and the likelihood of locating prints suitable for identification purposes. The possibility of success decreases as the amount of time increases.

The physical makeup of the person leaving the imprint is also important. People with rough skin and people with a propensity to sweat can be expected to leave more residue on any surface with which they make contact; for this reason, the imprint is likely to last longer and be more pronounced. Prints that have been directly exposed to meteorological phenomena such as rain or snow are unlikely to produce good results.

Comparison With Known Standards or Standards for Comparison

Known standards or standards for comparison (discussed in chapter 11) are necessary for determining who has made the fingerprints. Where fingerprints have been taken by the police from a suspect or accused charged with an indictable offence, the comparison procedure is less involved, because a one-to-one comparison is possible. Otherwise, the police need to search for comparable prints.

Under the authority of the *Identification of Criminals Act*, the police are authorized to fingerprint and photograph any individual arrested for or charged with an indictable offence. The fingerprints are sent to a central repository administered and staffed by the RCMP in Ottawa. This repository keeps a record of the fingerprints of everyone who has been charged with or convicted of an indictable offence in Canada. It acts as the search-and-comparison site for police to determine the possible identity of persons involved in a crime. Fingerprints lifted from a crime scene are photographed and sent to the RCMP facility for comparison. If an individual has his or her prints on file as a result of a previous arrest or conviction, a comparison will be made with the prints submitted by the police and the individual's identity will be determined. This comparison is made by examining the characteristics of each print. When sufficient identical characteristics are noted (usually 10 to 12 points of comparison), an expert will give his or her opinion that the print submitted is that of the individual whose prints are on file. As previously stated, fingerprint identifications by experts are seldom successfully challenged by the defence.

The Potential of Fingerprint Identification

The identification of an accused's fingerprints at a crime scene does not in and of itself indicate that the accused committed the crime. An identified fingerprint can prove only that the maker of that fingerprint was once at the crime scene. When the accused denies being at the scene or it can be shown that the accused normally would not have had access to the scene, finding a fingerprint places an onus on the accused to explain how the print got there. Fingerprint evidence is circumstantial and requires additional proof by the Crown as to the significance of the print and how it got there. Fingerprints cannot be used to prove intent or consciousness of guilt; however, they can be used to corroborate eyewitness testimony and other evidence. Unfortunately, when a fingerprint was made cannot be determined by experts.

The fingerprint of an accused found on an object used to commit a crime is also circumstantial evidence. The fingerprint of an accused found on a discarded weapon used in the commission of a homicide is proof only that the accused had that weapon in his or her possession at some point. The Crown is required to prove that the accused's possession of the weapon was related to the commission of the offence. If an accused's fingerprints are found at a crime scene to which the accused did not have legitimate access, they may establish a *prima facie* case when they point to no logical conclusion other than that the accused is guilty. Consider, for example, a robbery investigation in which the police are advised by the cashier that he was robbed at gunpoint by a person wearing a ski mask and hat. The cashier advises the police that he could not identify the robber because of the disguise. The cashier further advises that the robber went behind the sales counter, opened the cash register by punching the correct key sequence, and reached into the drawer to remove the money. Police identification experts are successful in lifting a print identified as belonging to the accused from the drawer and one side of the cash register. In this case, the accused may be found guilty on this evidence alone, as no logical conclusion is possible other than that the accused committed the crime.

In cases where the fingerprints of an accused are found on an object that has been removed from a crime scene but not found in the possession or control of the accused, the fingerprints can be used to prove, circumstantially, that the accused at one time came into contact with the object. The Crown is left with the burden of proving that the accused came into contact with this object through illegitimate means.

Stolen property that cannot otherwise be identified by its owner may be proved to be the owner's property by identifying the owner's fingerprints on the property. Fingerprints can also corroborate the sworn testimony of a victim who states that he or she was at a particular place. Of course, although the victim's location can be confirmed by fingerprints, one cannot know when the prints were made.

Fingerprints can also be used to rule out particular individuals as suspects. When suspects supply fingerprints to police officers, a comparison of their prints with prints found at the crime scene may be undertaken; if the prints do not match, the individual may be eliminated as a suspect.

Shoeprints and Tire Impressions

Just as a tool will leave an impression when it comes into contact with a softer substance, so does a shoe or tire leave an impression in soft soil, clay, mud, or snow. Shoes and tires also leave an imprint on hard surfaces when the surface is covered with some type of residue or there is dirt or oil on the shoe or tire itself. When contact is made with a shoe or tire, the imprint is detectable only when the surface with which the shoe or tire made contact is smooth or polished. A linoleum floor will usually receive prints from a soiled shoe or tire, while an irregular cement surface will not, unless the cement is highly polished. A shoe or tire that has come into contact with a liquid such as paint, oil, or water will leave a detectable impression on a hard surface with which it subsequently comes into contact.

Prints made by shoes or tires in soft substances can be lifted by adding a plaster-like material to a bounded area around the impression. Once hardened, the plaster produces a mould of the impression that allows the pattern of the shoe or tire to be compared with known standards from shoe or tire companies. The mould will not only indicate the manufacturer of the product but also produce identifiable characteristics identical to those of the shoe or tire producing the impression. The same holds true for imprints left by residue when a shoe or tire comes into contact with a hard, smooth surface. Imprints left on hard, smooth surfaces are often difficult to see and require a light dusting of powder before they can be photographed by forensic experts. Expert examination of prints from shoes and tires often results in positive identification of the prints and seizure of the objects that made them.

The Potential Evidentiary Value of Prints Made by Shoes and Tires

Impressions or prints made by shoes and tires can link an accused to a crime scene. They may allow an expert to state that the person wearing the shoe or driving the car in question was at the scene. While opinions of this kind cannot establish a *prima facie* case, they often corroborate eyewitness testimony.

In addition to placing an accused at the scene of a crime, shoe and tire impressions can, when viewed by experts, supply the investigator with a wealth of information regarding the offender and the method used to commit the offence. Depending on the number of shoeprints found, one may be able to determine the approximate height and weight of the offender, the speed at which he or she was walking or running, whether there were abnormalities in the offender's stride, and whether the offender was carrying a heavy load such as a body. When tire impressions are examined by experts, it may be possible to determine the vehicle's direction of travel and the number of passengers in the vehicle.

In cases where it is impossible to bring the actual print or the surface on which the print was discovered to court, the *Canada Evidence Act* provides for the use of photographs.

WRITINGS AND DOCUMENTS

When examined by experts, documents printed on a typewriter or cheque machine can be linked to the machine that made them. When a document is part of a criminal act, linking the equipment that printed the document to the document, and thus to the owner of the equipment, is of the utmost importance. Cases involving ransom notes, frauds, and false pretenses are crimes that may require document examination.

Handwritten documents should also be examined by experts to determine the source of the handwriting. Suicide notes and the like should be examined with the intention of identifying the handwriting as being that of the victim. When a link with the supposed suicide victim is doubtful or impossible to establish, the possibility of homicide arises. In cases where a document is partially destroyed by fire, chemical processing of the document by experts may reveal what was written on the document. Expert examination often reveals what was written on a notepad even when all that remains are indentations.

TRACE ELEMENTS

trace elements
chemical/biological substances in tiny quantities

Dirt, dust, and residue, even in the minutest quantities, may prove significant to a case. Minute quantities of materials are referred to as **trace elements** and should be examined by experts when found at the scene of a crime. The possible point of origin of these elements can be determined, and possibly link an accused to the crime or crime scene. Examination of paint or glass found at the scene of a hit-and-run may be linked to a suspect vehicle. Glass and paint may be traced to a manufacturer, thus leading to the identification of a suspect vehicle and consequently to the suspect. Wood or other materials at an arson scene may produce trace elements of the accelerant used to start or maintain the fire. Further examination by experts may uncover a specific chemical composition of the fluid, thus linking it to a suspect possessing the same material. During an investigation into a series of arson fires in Hamilton, experts linked the flammable fluid used to start the fires to fluid in the garage of one of the suspects. The chemicals the fluid used to commit the crime and in the fluid in the garage were mixed in exactly the same proportions. As well, that particular mix was not sold by any manufacturer.

The transfer of trace elements such as hair and fibres from a perpetrator to a victim or vice versa is common in crimes such as homicide, aggravated assault, and kidnapping. Finding hair as a trace element on either the accused or the victim links the two individuals. Although hair cannot positively identify an accused unless accompanied by DNA testing, expert analysis may reveal much about the originator of the hair if the hair sample is complete—that is, if it contains the root, shaft, and tip. Analysis can reveal racial background, the area of the body from which the hair originated, whether the hair was dyed or bleached, the presence of foreign oils or other hair treatments, and whether the hair was permed. Blood type may be determined by examining the root.

Expert examination of fibres may determine the point of origin or manufacturer of the item from which they came. Forensic examination of fibres may enable an expert to state that the fibres found at a crime scene were the same as those found on a suspect. During the Atlanta child murder investigation of the 1970s, experts were able to determine that fibres found on the soles of the shoes of one of the victims were left behind after contact between the victim and a rug in the accused's residence. The accused stated that the victim had never been at his residence.

BODILY FLUIDS: BLOOD, SEMEN, AND URINE

DNA testing, with its unequalled ability to identify the source of samples, has largely superseded traditional testing of bodily fluids. However, examination of bodily fluids in specific investigations still remains important.

Blood

The evidentiary value of blood is paramount in impaired driving cases where a blood sample is available. Determining the percentage of alcohol in the suspect's blood is one of the key factors in an impaired driving charge. In cases where an accused's sobriety, and therefore his or her ability to formulate intent, are at issue, an examination by experts may influence the outcome of the trial.

Expert examination can also tell investigators whether an unknown substance is indeed human blood. This, of course, can be an important investigative step in determining whether violence occurred at a crime scene. However, non-DNA blood analysis cannot identify the specific person to whom the blood belonged, although it can identify his or her blood group.

An understanding of the **hydrodynamics** (fluid motion) of blood can be extremely valuable to an investigator. Because it is a fluid, blood conforms to the laws that govern the motion and properties of other fluids. Understanding hydrodynamics allows the investigator to reach conclusions that are pertinent to crime scene investigations.

A study of the size and shape of blood drops on a floor can indicate the height from which they fell and thus the possible location of the wound producing the drops. The shape of the drop may indicate movement by the source of the drop. A person who is in motion while bleeding

hydrodynamics
the movement properties of water/liquids

will produce a tear-shaped drop with a narrow end indicating the direction of travel (the rounded end points toward the bleeder). An examination of bloodspatter on a wall may indicate the force and direction of the blow that caused the blood to spatter. It may also indicate how far the victim was from the wall when the wound was made.

Semen

Investigations of sexual assault often require an examination of semen found on or in the victim or at the suspected crime scene. A forensic determination that a fluid is indeed semen may assist in proving a claim that sexual intercourse took place. The presence of sperm in its live (motile) state supports the identification of a collected sample as semen. Samples of fluid taken from the vagina may remain identifiable as containing semen for up to several days. DNA testing of sperm can identify the individual responsible for the test sample. Vaginal fluid samples from a complainant in a sexual assault case are taken by a physician, who then turns the sample over to the police for laboratory analysis.

Urine

urinalysis
microscopic and/or chemical analysis of the composition of urine

Laboratory analysis of urine is of limited value because it cannot be used to identify a specific individual. **Urinalysis** can, however, determine the amount of alcohol in the blood and, more important, detect poisons in the body. Urinalysis can also indicate whether a suspect has a particular illness such as diabetes.

DNA TESTING

Of all the breakthroughs in forensic science, none, with the possible exception of fingerprint identification, is more effective than DNA analysis in attempting to identify the perpetrator of a crime. All human beings have a distinctive genetic code within their 46 chromosomes. These chromosomes are composed of **deoxyribonucleic acid (DNA)**.

deoxyribonucleic acid (DNA)
a biological compound that forms cell chromosomes and from which genetic information can be gleaned

Laboratory analysis of blood stains, semen, saliva, vaginal secretions, skin, and hair follicles can lead to the identification of an individual through his or her distinctive genetic code. These substances, which may be found at a crime scene or on or in a victim or suspect, can positively identify an individual with a certainty exceeding one in several billion.

The advantages of DNA testing are without equal, whereas the disadvantages are few. Minute samples of human material are sufficient to produce good results even when a sample may be a combination of two or more substances. For example, a semen sample taken from the vagina of a sexual assault complainant may have blood mixed with it. The source of the blood may be either the victim or the suspect, yet this apparent contamination does not affect the reliability of the test. The identity of the assailant will be revealed by DNA testing of the semen.

DNA testing can also rule out suspects, thereby reducing the risk of a miscarriage of justice.

However, the need for a sample from the suspect to compare with the substance taken from the victim or found at the crime scene severely limits the application of this scientific advance. Because DNA testing is in its infancy and much case law remains to be made, the law surrounding the collection of comparison samples from suspects remains unclear.

The courts have noted on several occasions that the use of bodily fluids and other substances obtained from suspects without their consent is a serious violation of s. 8 of the *Canadian Charter of Rights and Freedoms* (see *R v. Dyment*, 1988). Where a sample is given by consent, the consent must be informed, meaning that the accused has been fully informed of his or her rights under ss. 10(a) and 10(b) of the Charter. The consent must not be coerced or gained by trickery and deceit.

In July 1995 the law was changed to allow search warrants for obtaining certain bodily substances from suspects for DNA testing. The *Criminal Code* now allows the court to issue a search warrant authorizing the police to take samples of hair, saliva, and blood in connection with offences listed in s. 487.04. The criteria are set out in s. 487.05 and the procedures are described in s. 487.06. Application for a warrant is made *ex parte* to a Provincial Court judge as defined in s. 487.04.

ex parte
(Latin) a legal proceeding decided in the absence of one of the parties likely to be affected by its result is said to be ex parte

GUNSHOT RESIDUE

When a firearm is discharged, many materials other than the projectile are expelled from the muzzle. These materials—**gunshot residue (GSR)**—include gases, unburned or partially burned powder grains, carbon particles, traces of the bullet lubricant, traces of primer components (lead, barium, nitrates), fragments of soft bullets (lead, antimony), fragments of the bullet jacket, and metal traces from the cartridge case or gun barrel. These trace elements are deposited on the hands of the person discharging the gun and are, under certain circumstances, detectable and identifiable.

gunshot residue (GSR)
trace substances left on surfaces (including the hand of the shooter) after the discharge of a firearm

A procedure known as the **paraffin test** was used at one time to detect GSR; however, because of its lack of specificity, this test has been replaced by a chemical **handwash test**. The handwash test requires the suspect to wash his or her hands in a chemical solution that is then sent to the laboratory for analysis. The test is able to detect elevated levels of lead, barium, and antimony, which may indicate that the suspect fired a gun recently. However, handling a weapon after it has been fired may contaminate the hands, thus leading to an incorrect conclusion.

paraffin test
an obsolete test/collection method for gunshot residue

handwash test
a procedure in current use for the collection of gunshot residue evidence; it involves a suspect washing his or her hands in a substance containing chemical reagents

While GSR chemicals may be found in elevated amounts on a suspect, this fact alone is an insufficient basis for concluding that the suspect fired the weapon used in the commission of the offence being investigated. The GSR test cannot determine the time at which the suspect may have fired the gun or whether the gun fired was that which caused the wound. The GSR test is less effective when the time between firing the gun and taking the handwash sample exceeds four hours.

scanning electron microscopy (SEM) test

a newer method of interpreting gunshot residue evidence that requires a collection method less cumbersome than the chemical handwash

A more recent test for GSR shows great promise. **Scanning electron microscopy (SEM) test** procedures, which provide results that appear to be more accurate and consistent than the handwash test, also require a sample from the suspect, but taking the sample is less cumbersome. A special utensil containing a gummed substance is held against the skin and then removed. The GSR adheres to the gummed substance, which is then prepared for examination by the scanning electron microscope.

FIREARM AND PROJECTILE EXAMINATION

In its own way, each bullet fired from a gun keeps a diary of where it has been and what it has done. The bullet's base will have irregular dimples marking the pressure delivered there in the bullet's acceleration through the barrel of the gun. The bullet's sides will bear the markings of the barrel's spiral rifling. These markings will reflect microscopic imperfections in the gun, and can be as specific as a fingerprint.

Forensic specialists can determine with certainty that a recovered bullet was fired from a particular gun when the bullet is compared with the suspect weapon. The specialist's ability to identify the gun depends on the bullet's condition.

An examination of the cartridge can identify the type of weapon from which a bullet was fired, including the make and model. Comparisons of multiple cartridges or shell-casings can result in a finding that they were all fired from the same weapon. A microscopic examination of slide marks on the casings can identify whether the marks were made by the same breach or the firing pin of the weapon creating the same indentation in each cartridge.

A forensic expert's statement that a projectile or bullet was fired by a particular gun creates a very strong case against the owner or possessor of the gun. There have been instances in which experts were able to isolate and successfully identify a suspect's fingerprint on a cartridge, thereby proving that the suspect was in possession of the firearm at the location where the casing was found.

Each firearm sold has a manufacturer's serial number stamped into it, which may be used to identify the weapon. Firearms registration allows gun ownership to be traced. It should be noted that attempts may be made to obliterate or change the weapon's serial number. Expert examination can identify gun oils and solvents used to clean a weapon, making it possible to match these substances to traces found on ammunition.

BITE MARKS

Bite marks are often found in sexual assaults and homicides and can be matched to the individual who inflicted the bite. The bite marks are photographed by experts and compared with the suspect's teeth. Casts are made from bite marks left in flesh and other soft surfaces. Bite marks faded by the passage of time can be enhanced by ultraviolet light.

BROKEN NAILS

Like bullets, each person's fingernails have distinctive striations (grooves or channels). Broken fingernails found at a crime scene can be matched to the person they came from many months after the crime has been committed. Known samples from the suspect are needed for comparison.

FRACTURE MATCHES

Fracture matches can link broken pieces of material at a crime scene to pieces of the material found on a suspect. Expert examination of material torn away from its original source can lead to a positive match. Glass found at the scene of a hit-and-run can be matched to the headlight from which it originated. A burnt match found at a crime scene may be identified as having been torn from a book of paper matches found on a suspect.

GLASS

Broken glass found at a crime scene may be significant evidence. As stated above, glass can be matched to its original source. Glass can also assist in reconstructing the crime. Experts who examine broken glass are able to determine the impact side of the glass and, by studying the break pattern determine the size of the instrument used to break the glass and how much force was used. Although most glass moves in the direction of the force that causes it to break, shards may be found on the person who applied the force.

An examination of projectile holes in glass may reveal the sequence in which the holes were made. The sequence is revealed by the radial and concentric break lines around the hole.

An examination of glass at the scene of a suspected break-and-enter is often necessary for determining whether a break-and-enter actually occurred or was merely staged to provide cover for other activities.

KEY TERMS

transference

latent fingerprint

trace elements

hydrodynamics

urinalysis

deoxyribonucleic acid (DNA)

ex parte

gunshot residue (GSR)

paraffin test

handwash test

scanning electron microscopy
   (SEM) test

REVIEW

■ **SHORT ANSWER**

1. "Physical evidence is more reliable than eyewitness testimony and therefore has a higher evidentiary value." Provide a justification for this statement.

2. What is the evidentiary value of linking a tool impression found at a crime scene with a tool found in a suspect's possession?

3. How can the link described in question 2 be made by police and forensic experts?

4. Why are fingerprints an excellent way to identify an individual?

5. What are "latent fingerprints"? How do they differ from the other two types of fingerprints?

6. What is the evidentiary value of finding an accused's fingerprints at a crime scene? Can the fingerprints allow one to determine when the crime was committed?

7. What factors affect the discovery and quality of latent fingerprints?

8. A shoeprint is found in soft mud at the scene of a break-and-enter, beneath the window used to gain entry to the residence. Experts identify the impression as having been made by a shoe worn by the accused. Explain the potential evidentiary value of the print.

9. How are paint chips and glass found on the victim of a hit-and-run significant to the investigation of that crime?

10. Explain how an understanding of the hydrodynamics of blood can be useful to an investigator reconstructing a homicide scene at which copious amounts of the victim's blood are found. What may be proved by an examination of the bloodspatter patterns?

11. Describe the evidentiary potential of semen stains found on the clothing and person of a victim of a sexual assault. Can the identity of the perpetrator be established if his semen is found on or near the victim? Explain.

12. Discuss the advantages and disadvantages of DNA evidence and testing.

13. Explain the process used in linking a bullet to the gun that fired it.

14. How can an examination of window glass found at the scene of a crime assist in the reconstruction of that crime?

■ TRUE OR FALSE?

_____ 1. An examination by experts can determine the age of a fingerprint.

_____ 2. Identifying a blood sample's blood group is sufficient to identify an accused.

_____ 3. The impact side of a pane of glass may be determined by expert examination of pieces of glass taken from the pane.

_____ 4. A broken fingernail found at a crime scene can be matched to a specific individual.

_____ 5. There is no legal provision for taking a sample of blood from a person for DNA testing.

_____ 6. Urinalysis can determine the identity of the donor.

CHAPTER 13

The Investigation of Sudden Death

CHAPTER OBJECTIVES

After completing this chapter, you should be able to:

◆ Describe the kinds of evidence that point to homicide and suicide in sudden death investigations.

◆ Describe how time of death is established in sudden death investigations.

◆ Describe the most common causes of unnatural death.

INTRODUCTION

The investigation of sudden death is seldom left to the inexperienced police officer and demands the attention of a seasoned investigator. In Ontario the larger police departments rely on a special **homicide team/ squad** to conduct sudden death investigations.

This chapter is not designed as an abridged course in homicide investigation. Its purpose is to give potential police officer candidates an overview of what they may expect to find at the scene of a suicide, homicide, or accidental or premature death, and to describe the potential of various investigative methods associated with sudden death investigations. In addition, the chapter includes information on signs that may indicate cause of death.

Erroneous conclusions drawn by police officers on viewing the scene of a sudden death have far-reaching effects. If a sudden death is treated as a suicide as opposed to a homicide because of a misinterpretation of the crime scene, the result may be destruction of evidence and a serious miscarriage of justice.

homicide team/squad
a team of police officers with special training in the investigation of homicide and suspicious death

THE CHRONOLOGY OF ASSUMPTIONS

The following scenario is uncommon but still encountered frequently enough that it can be used to demonstrate an important point.

The police receive a 911 call to investigate what appears to be a dead body on the sidewalk adjacent to a 12-storey apartment building. On arrival, the officers note the body of a man lying face down in a large pool of blood on the sidewalk. Checking for signs of life, the officers find none. A witness states that he heard something hit the sidewalk about 10 feet behind him. Turning around, he saw the man whose body is now being checked by the police.

There are a number of possible explanations for how the victim got to where he was found. On looking up to the 12th floor, the police notice an open window with a curtain blowing through the opening. What should the police conclude from the evidence?

1. The man committed suicide by jumping to his death from the 12th floor.

2. The man died as a result of an accidental fall from the 12th floor.

3. The man was the victim of a homicide and was pushed from the 12th-floor window.

4. The man was the victim of a homicide made to look like a suicide.

If the officers misinterpret the scene, the possibility of evidence destruction becomes very high. As was noted in chapter 11, unprotected crime scenes become contaminated or are destroyed. To reduce the likelihood of this happening, only one assumption should be made—the **worst-case scenario**. Assuming that a homicide has occurred creates the least opportunity for the destruction of evidence.

worst-case scenario
an investigative hypothesis that involves basing one's research or actions on the initial assumption that the "worst case" (from the standpoint of legal responsibility) has occurred

Working from the premise that the man was a homicide victim, the police continue their investigation until this possibility is eliminated by the evidence. The police then treat the incident as a suicide until the evidence eliminates that possibility. When homicide and suicide have been eliminated, the police conclude that death was accidental. An officer's ability to fully investigate these hypotheses depends on a solid grounding in the interpretation of evidence.

EVIDENCE INDICATING HOMICIDE

Evidence at the scene of a possible homicide must support the hypothesis that death was the result of a criminal act.

Homicides are acts of violence visited on a person (the victim) by one or more other persons (the suspects) that result in the victim's death. A visible wound is the type of evidence that most often indicates an act of violence. The position and number of wounds may indicate homicide or suicide. Multiple wounds are a good indicator of homicide. If the position or location of the wound is such that it could not have been caused by the victim, the wound was probably caused by someone else (indicating homicide).

The condition of the scene will often alert the police to the possibility of homicide. Overturned or broken furniture may indicate a struggle or violent action. Forcible entry of a room, apartment, or house may suggest homicide. If the victim is found outdoors, trampled grass, broken or bent shrubs, dirt or mud on the clothing and person of the victim, or the inaccessibility of the area in which the victim was found may indicate homicide.

Short of a description of the incident by a witness, the most notable indication of homicide is a wound coupled with the absence of a weapon capable of causing the wound. In addition, the absence of a wallet or cash and credit cards on the body may indicate robbery and thus the possibility of homicide.

In some cases where the evidence does not clearly point to a cause of death, the police require a report by a **pathologist** to confirm cause of death. A report noting internal signs of sexual assault or other kinds of violence, or the presence of poisons or narcotics in the system, may indicate homicide.

pathologist
a scientist/doctor specializing in the study of the causes of disease and death

When all of the above-noted evidence is considered and found to be absent, the police should assume suicide.

EVIDENCE INDICATING SUICIDE

Evidence at the scene of a possible suicide must support the hypothesis that death was the result of an act of violence by the victim himself or herself without assistance from another.

Death by suicide is sometimes accompanied by a handwritten note left at or near the scene by the victim. To determine whether the note was written by the victim, handwriting analysis and the opinions of people who had personal knowledge of the victim's handwriting should be relied on. When the handwriting is that of the victim, the suicide note, if it is substantiated by other facts, can be a strong indicator of suicide. Notes made on a typewriter or computer are far less reliable. Even when the typing on the note can be linked to a machine to which the victim had access, the note's authorship and the conditions under which the note was typed remain unknown.

People seldom take their own lives without a reason. As rational beings we might view suicide as not an option in a particular set of circumstances, but to a person who is suffering great physical pain, mental anguish, or extreme depression it may appear to be the only option. Motives for suicide can be related to, among other things, personal finances, parent-child relationships, love interests, legal problems, marriage difficulties, and physical or mental health problems. In the case of young people, scholastic problems must also be considered. Questioning friends, co-workers, and spouses, children and other family members may uncover a motive for suicide.

Just as the absence of a weapon capable of causing a wound found on the body is an indicator of homicide, the close proximity to the body of a weapon capable of causing the wound may indicate suicide. To support a conclusion of suicide, evidence must exist to indicate that the wound is located and was caused in such a way that it could have been the result of action by the victim. The possibility always exists that someone is attempting to cover up a homicide by disguising it as suicide.

If the pathologist conducting the autopsy reports that the victim died of an overdose, and that the narcotic which caused death was the same as a narcotic prescribed to and previously taken by the victim, the finding provides a reliable indicator of suicide. Past suicide attempts by the victim may further suggest suicide as the cause of death.

An absence of evidence pointing to homicide or suicide allows these to be eliminated as causes of death, and allows investigators to assume that death was the result of an accident or natural causes.

QUESTIONS TO BE ANSWERED BY THE INVESTIGATION

All sudden deaths can be placed into one of four categories: homicide, suicide, accidental death, or death from natural causes. But whatever the classification, certain basic questions need to be answered at the conclusion of any sudden death investigation. Every effort is made to conduct the investigation in such a way that these questions are answered.

Identifying the Victim: Who Died?

In most cases identifying the victim is not a problem. Parents, other family members, co-workers, and friends of the victim are all sources for identification. Identification of the deceased should, nevertheless, be corroborated in other ways. Personal identification found on the victim (such as a driver's licence, a social insurance card, and credit cards) may be used to corroborate other forms of identification.

In the rare instances where the victim is unknown, fingerprints or DNA testing may be used for identification, assuming there is a known sample with which to make a comparison. In extreme cases where decomposition or injury-related disfigurement make visual identification impossible, dental records or x rays may corroborate a tentative identification. Surgical scars and tattoos may assist in developing leads to people who may have an intimate knowledge of the victim.

Estimating the Time of Death: When Did Death Occur?

When death occurred is of concern to the police regardless of the kind of death. In homicide, establishing the time of death narrows the scope of the investigation by reducing the number of suspects who would have had an opportunity to commit the offence. Establishing the time of death of a suicide victim may help to suggest witnesses with information related to the physical or mental condition of the victim. In cases of accidental or natural death a determination of the time of death may be required to assist the family with insurance or pension claims.

It is generally accepted that both the police and the pathologist are responsible for establishing the time of death. The police interview witnesses with the intention of establishing the time of death, and the pathologist establishes or confirms the time of death through the autopsy. There are a number of procedures that a pathologist may use at the scene or during the autopsy itself to determine the time of death.

Body Temperature

Though body temperature cooling is not considered an accurate way to judge time of death, it may be used in conjunction with other approaches. A dead body eventually assumes the temperature of the room or other environment in which is it located. By comparing the environmental temperature with the body's temperature (taken rectally), the approximate number of hours since death can be determined. Body temperature drops 2 to 3 degrees in the first hour after death and 1 to 1.5 degrees each hour thereafter. These amounts may vary in extreme weather conditions. In addition, body temperature drops more slowly in obese persons, if the victim had a fever, or if the victim was strenuously exercising or had just completed strenuous exercise.

Rigor Mortis

Rigor mortis, which is caused by enzyme breakdown, is a stiffening of the entire body after death. It begins in the face and head about 6 hours after death and reaches the feet within 12 to 18 hours of death. It starts to leave the body, beginning with the face and head, 24 hours after death, and is gone by the 36-hour mark. A number of factors can affect the timing of each phase: strenuous exercise before death, the deceased's muscular development, and temperature changes in the body's surroundings.

rigor mortis
a temporary stiffening of the body after death due to an enzymatic reaction

Post Mortem Lividity

When the heart stops beating at death, the blood stops circulating through the body and gravity causes the blood to settle in the lowest areas of the body, which as a result turn a deep purple. This is known as **post mortem lividity**. Unless the body is moved, the purple areas should be the areas nearest the ground. Post mortem lividity requires about five to eight hours to fully set in. Once it sets in it will not change, even if the body is moved. If a body is found face down on the floor, post mortem lividity should be clearly visible on the face and elsewhere on the front of the body. If five hours have passed since death and the body is moved and placed on its back, post mortem lividity will not change; accordingly, finding a body on its back, but with post mortem lividity on its front, indicates that the body has been moved since death occurred.

post mortem lividity
a discolouration of certain parts of the body after death due to pooling of blood after circulation has ceased

Areas of the body that are pressed tight against an object such as a floor will remain white because the blood vessels are constricted and incapable of absorbing blood. In other areas of the body where the flesh is compressed (such as under a wrist-watch), post mortem lividity will not be present, once again because of the inability of the constricted vessels to absorb blood.

Despite the several tests available to medical science for judging time of death, trying to determine when someone died is an inaccurate exercise unless it is supported by other evidence. It is therefore important to have witnesses who can attest to the victim's habits or provide a last sighting of the victim.

Establishing the Location: Where Did Death Occur?

Establishing where death occurred is pertinent to all sudden death investigations. In the vast majority of cases, death will have occurred where the body is located; on rare occasions, however, the body will have been moved in an attempt to disguise the nature of the death. A homicide may be made to look like a suicide or an accidental death by moving the body from the original crime scene. Where newborns are concerned, it sometimes happens that the body is found not where the child was born but where his or her body was abandoned.

Like establishing the time of death, establishing where death occurred reduces the number of suspects. Determining that a body has been moved and ascertaining the location of death help the police locate witnesses to the death. It is also of paramount importance to find the location of death so that physical evidence can be obtained. Only rarely can a pathologist help determine the location of death. The hope that in drowning cases an examination by a pathologist of the water contained in the lungs can identify where the victim drowned is largely unrealized.

An absence of physical evidence is usually the best indicator that a body has been moved. If the body is moved five to eight hours or more after death, the signs of post mortem lividity may indicate that the position of the body within that time was not the same as the position in which the body is found. This should immediately give rise to suspicion on the part of the police.

Establishing the Cause of Death: How Did Death Occur?

All death occurs as a result of one of three mechanisms: the body loses its blood in a quantity sufficient to cause death, the heart stops pumping blood, or respiration stops. The investigation of sudden death includes, in large part, a discovery of the manner in which one or more of the above mechanisms of death occurred. Was death a result of homicide, suicide, accident, or natural causes?

Police investigation of the death scene, police interpretation of physical evidence, police interviewing of witnesses, and the post mortem examination (**autopsy**) by the pathologist all help determine whether death was a result of homicide, suicide, accident, or natural causes. The pathologist's determination of the mechanism and manner of death should coincide with evidence collected by the police.

autopsy
an examination of a dead body made to determine such issues as the cause and time of death; a post mortem examination

Evidence Related to Cause of Death

The most common causes of unnatural death, some of which are discussed below, include gunshot wounds, stabbing or cutting wounds, blows from blunt instruments, asphyxia (choking), drowning, hanging, smothering, strangulation, poisoning, burning, electric shock, and lightning. Each of these mechanisms is associated with specific forensic clues or evidence.

Gunshot Wounds

The major mechanism of death associated with gunshot wounds is internal hemorrhaging. The size and velocity of the ammunition determines the degree of damage to the body. Shots fired from a distance leave little or no telltale residue on the skin, but if the muzzle is in direct contact with or near the skin a contact wound will be evident. A muzzle impression will be visible where there is contact with the skin, and if the weapon is fired at close range, soot and residue will be visible around the wound. The entry wound is normally smaller than the bullet because of the elasticity of the skin; this wound displays a gray to black abrasion collar. An exit wound is normally larger and jagged, and no abrasion is visible.

Stab Wounds and Cutting Wounds

Stab wounds are caused by a thrusting action. The major damage in stab wounds is to internal tissues; there is also damage caused by internal and external bleeding. In most cases the cause of death is blood loss rather than damage to a vital organ. The majority of stabbing deaths are murders; death can be caused by a single wound or multiple wounds. Defensive wounds, found on the hands, arms, and legs, are the result of a victim's attempts to fend off his or her assailant. In cases of cutting, external bleeding is generally the cause of death. Cutting wounds are frequently found in suicides. It is common in these cases to observe hesitation marks in the area of the main wound. These cuts are less severe and reflect the building up of sufficient courage to inflict the main wound.

Asphyxia

Asphyxia results when the brain and tissues receive insufficient oxygen to support the red blood cells. A pathologist's examination of the blood cells will disclose this condition. Although discolouration is common in all dead bodies, in asphyxiated victims the colour is more pronounced, particularly in the facial area, because of the lack of oxygen. Death by asphyxiation can be the result of choking, drowning, smothering, hanging, strangulation, or poisoning.

asphyxia
marked and potentially fatal deprivation of oxygen flow to body tissues (including the brain), usually due to a breathing obstruction

Drowning

The vast majority of drowning deaths are accidents or suicides. If a dead body is placed in water in an attempt to disguise a murder, the pathologist will discover the deception, for no water will be present in the victim's lungs.

Hanging

Although hangings are usually suicides, murders have been made to appear as suicides by hanging. Some hangings result from attempts at sexual gratification. Death by hanging occurs because the air supply is restricted, not because of a broken neck, as might be thought. In hangings, the ligature marks start from the area of the neck below the chin and travel upward to a point just below the ears. In investigations of death by hanging, the police should save the rope, including the knot.

Strangulation

Strangulation by rope, hands, or wire produces the same effects as hanging. Again, death results from a restriction of the air supply. Ligature marks caused by strangulation are normally evenly grooved and horizontal around the neck. In cases of manual strangulation, marks produced by hand pressure are often still visible.

Poisoning

Poisoning can be present in accidents, suicides, and homicides. It can occur when a large dose of poison is taken all at once or be the result of an accumulation of small doses over time. Poisons can be injected, ingested, inhaled, or absorbed through the skin. A toxicology examination can determine the amount and type of poison. Checking the victim's medicine cabinet or consulting the victim's pharmacy can help establish how the victim came into contact with the poison.

Burning

Most deaths by burning are accidental; deaths resulting from arson are classed as homicides. Some criminals try to make homicides look like accidental burnings. Considerable information can be gleaned from an autopsy. Carbon monoxide testing of the body allows the pathologist to determine whether the victim was dead before the fire occurred. In intense fires, breaks in the flesh may look like stab wounds. A pathologist can determine whether the breaks are true wounds.

CONCLUSION

The material in this chapter is designed to familiarize the novice police officer with situations he or she may encounter when called to the scene of a sudden death. This chapter is not meant to suggest that the novice officer, after reading the material, will be equipped to handle a complex sudden death investigation, especially in cases of homicide.

A novice officer who has a fundamental knowledge of the situations he or she is likely to encounter at the scene of a sudden death is far less likely to act in a manner or employ techniques that will destroy evidence or otherwise compromise an investigation. An officer who attends the scene of a sudden death must understand that he or she should never disturb the body. Furthermore, until the victim is pronounced dead by a physician, an investigating officer should always assume that the victim may still be alive. This precaution, obviously, may be ignored when the body is decapitated or decomposed, or when rigor mortis is present.

KEY TERMS

homicide team/squad

worst-case scenario

pathologist

rigor mortis

post mortem lividity

autopsy

asphyxia

REVIEW

■ SHORT ANSWER

1. On attending a call to investigate a sudden death, the police should always assume the worst-case scenario. Explain what this means and why the assumption is justified.

2. How do the number and position of wounds help determine whether a sudden death was a homicide or a suicide?

3. Other than eyewitness testimony, what is the most notable evidence that a homicide has been committed?

4. Why do the police sometimes need a pathologist's report to determine whether a homicide has occurred?

5. The police, who have been called to a reported suicide, find the victim seated at a desk in his bedroom. There is an obvious bullet hole in his right temple and a revolver on the floor beside his chair. Is it reasonable for the police to treat the death as a suicide? Why?

6. At 8:00 p.m. the police arrive at the scene of a reported sudden death to find a man lying on his back on the floor. There are no signs of breathing, no pulse, and no heart beat. On examining the victim they find rigor mortis in the face and jaw only. What is the estimated time of death? Explain your answer.

7. On arrival at the scene of a reported sudden death, the police find a female victim about 25 years old lying on her back by the side door of her house. Post mortem lividity is noted on her face and elsewhere on the front of her body. What should the police conclude, and why?

8. Investigating a sudden death, the police locate the body of a man about 28 years old lying on his back in the living room of his house. The handle of what appears to be a hunting knife protrudes from the centre of his chest. On further investigation the police discover that the victim's computer is on. On the screen is a note indicating that the victim was about to commit suicide because of a failed relationship with his girlfriend. Is it reasonable at this point for the police to treat their inquiries as a suicide investigation? Explain your answer.

9. Explain the importance of establishing the time of death when investigating a homicide.

10. On attending the scene of a reported sudden death, you (a police officer) determine that the body has been moved. You make this determination because post mortem lividity is inconsistent with the position of the body. Why is the fact that the body was moved after death significant?

11. What is the major physiological cause of death associated with gunshot wounds?

12. On examining the body of a sudden death victim, you note what appears to be a bullet entry wound in the back of the head. The area of the scalp immediately surrounding the wound appears burnt and there is a noticeable amount of residue surrounding the wound. What conclusions might you draw from this examination?

13. What are defensive wounds?

14. Why should police officers investigating deaths by hanging save the rope, including the knot? (Research this question using sources outside this text.)

15. You discover a body immersed in a pond at the local golf course. At the autopsy you are advised by the pathologist that the victim's lungs contain little or no water. What conclusion can you draw from this information?

16. What is asphyxia?

APPENDIX

RCMP Investigator's Guide to Forensic Evidence, Second Edition

INTRODUCTION

This handbook has been produced for the police investigator as a guide for the collection of physical evidence at the scene. It may be used in one of two ways:

◆ By Type of Crime Scene

◆ By Type of Physical Evidence

Part I: Crime Scene—illustrates common crime scenes and evidence found thereat (number following item of evidence … indicates its location in Part II).

Part II: Type of Evidence—lists alphabetically types of physical evidence, collection and preservation of the exhibit and comparison standards required. Includes reference to the section of the Laboratory Services Manual to consult for more information.

For more detailed information about collection, packaging and transportation of exhibits, see the *Laboratory Services Manual*. Additional assistance is also available from your forensic laboratory.

Forensic Laboratory Vancouver	(604) 264-3400
Forensic Laboratory Edmonton	(403) 451-7400
Forensic Laboratory Regina	(306) 780-5807
Forensic Laboratory Winnipeg	(204) 983-5906
Central Forensic Laboratory (Ottawa)	(613) 998-6025
Forensic Laboratory Halifax	(902) 426-8886

PART I: COMMON CRIME SCENES

"A" Armed Robbery/Assault

◆ Ammunition (3)
(Imbedded shotgun pellets or fired bullets)

◆ Demand note
(Handwriting/handprinting) (35)

◆ Hair (34) and Fibres (25)

◆ Blood (5)

◆ Firearm (29)

◆ Clothing (14)

◆ Wound (76)

◆ Gunshot residue (33) and (14)

◆ Blood (5)

◆ Footwear (30)

◆ Fired & unfired ammunition (3)

Miscellaneous:

◆ Ammunition: Spent shotgun wadding; located in walls, floors, etc. (3)

◆ Fingerprints (27)

◆ Suspect's clothing (14)—refer to Scene "N"

◆ Mace, pepper spray (52)

"B" Arson

◆ Matches torn from matchbook (42)

◆ Accelerants (1)

◆ Debris from fire origin (28) (e.g. carpet, floor, sub-floor, soil, upholstery, etc.)

◆ Charred documents (11)

Miscellaneous:

◆ Comparison standards from uncontaminated areas

◆ Fingerprints (27)

◆ Soil (58)

◆ Suspect's clothing (14)—refer to Scene "N"

"C" Bombings

◆ Explosive devices (23)

◆ Explosive substances (24)

◆ Explosive debris (22)

Miscellaneous:

When the bombing results in death and/or substantial damage, contact the National Response Team member for assistance. Ottawa (613) 837-1772 or (613) 993-0886

"D" Break and Enter

- Glass samples from lightbulb and from broken window (32)
- Blood (5)
- Fibres (25)
- Paint (45)

- Toolmarks (65)
- Footwear impression (30)
- Tools (66)
- Matches (42)

Miscellaneous:

- Building products (8)
- Cigarette butts (13)
- Fingerprints (27)
- Paint (45)
- Safe insulation (54)

- Suspect's clothing (14)—refer to scene "N"
- Tape (61)
- Tiremarks (62)

"E" Counterfeiting Operations

Counterfeits can include currency, security documents and travel documents

"Printing Plant Search"

- Process camera
- Negatives
- Artwork
- Genuine documents
- Grey scale

- Dark room
  - Pieces of negatives
  - Negatives—Films
- Light table
- Artwork

Plate Burner

- Negatives on goldenrod paper
- Offset plates

- Negatives to be mounted on goldenrod paper

Press Area

- Printed sheets
- Image on impression cylinder
- Image on blanket

- Image on plate
- Scraps of paper

Paper Cutter

- Commercial style
- Manual style
- Uncut sheets of paper
- Paper trimmings with printed images

Garbage Cans

- Negatives
- Artwork
- Plates
- Paper

"F" Excise Act

Equipment

- Still containing wash (21)
- Worm (21)
- Receiver containing distilled product (21)
- Barrels of mash (21)
- Distilled product (21)

Miscellaneous:

- Fingerprints (27)

"G" Fraud/Forgery/Questioned Documents

In the field of Document Examination, the term "document" refers to any item containing visible or invisible markings that convey a message or meaning to someone. In this general sense, a document can include such things as marks on lumber, tattoos, marked cards, invisible inks, indentations on paper, etc.

- Rubber stamp impression (53)
- Chequewriter impressions (12)
- Typewriter (67)/Printer (51)
- Physical match (48)
- Alterations (2)
- Handwriting/Handprinting (35)
- Paper (46)
- Ink (37)
- Fingerprint (27)

Miscellaneous:

- Charred documents (11)
- Credit cards (17)
- Gambling devices (31)
- Paper matches (42)

- Photocopiers/photocopies (47)
- Price markers/labellers (50)
- Water-soaked documents (73)
- DNA evidence may be obtained from stamps and envelopes (55)
- Indented impressions (36)

Collection of Known Handwriting Standards

An ideal submission of known handwriting standards for comparison to questioned handwriting includes both *requested* and *collected* specimens. Refer to item (35) in Part II for more detailed information:

"Requested": refers to specimens prepared at the "request" of the investigator. The investigator should dictate to the writer the exact text as found on the questioned document(s).

"Collected": refers to specimens "collected" by the investigator from sources which depict a natural representation of the suspect's/complainant's writing. These are generally secured from normal day-to-day activities and include such things as business correspondence, cancelled cheques, personal letters, etc.

"H" Hit and Run

- Broken glass (32)
- Driver's blood (5), Hair (34)
- Paint chips (standard and foreign) (45)
- Blood (5), Hair (34), Fibres (25), & Tissue from victim (64)
- Broken lights (38)
- Vehicle parts (moulding, aerials, fenders, etc.) (70)
- Tiremarks (62)
- Broken glass (32), plastic lens, & car body parts (70)
- Blood (5)
- Paint (45)
- Victim's outer clothing (14)

Miscellaneous:

Comparison hair standards from victim and/or suspect (34)—refer to Scene "N"

"I" Homicide/Sudden Death

- Blood (5), Fibres (25), Hair (34), & GSR (33) on clothing (14) and weapon (74)

- Unknown liquid or powder (68)

- Drugs (20), Drug paraphernalia (19) & Medications/Chemicals (44)

- Knife (74)

- Handwriting (35)

- Suicide note

Miscellaneous:

- Ammunition (3)

- Autopsy exhibits—refer to Scene "M"

- Blood stain pattern (5)

- Fingerprints (27)

- Firearms (29)

- Intoxicants (68)

- Suspect's clothing (14)—refer to Scene "N"

- Tissue (64), Fibres (25) and blood under fingernails (26)

"J" Sexual Assault

Important: A sexual assault examination kit should be used for collection of evidence from the victim. (see Semen #56) Use Forensic Blood Collection Kit for alcohol/drug determinations. (see Blood #5, Urine #69)

- Blood (5)

- Seminal stains (56)

- Lubricant (40)

- Saliva (55)

- Fibres from scene (25) and clothing (14)

- Hair (34)

Miscellaneous:

- Blood (5), Tissue (64) and Fibres (25) under victim's fingernails (26)

- Liquid blood (5) and Saliva (55) samples from suspect

- Cigarette butts (13), Buttons (9) and torn fabric (14)

- Fingerprints (27)

- Sexual Assault Examination Kit (56)

- Suspect's belongings (60)

- Suspect's clothing (14)—refer to Scene "N"

- Unusual scene characteristics —e.g. paint chips, glass, liquor bottles, pill bottles

"K" Vehicle Theft

◆ Paint samples on stolen parts (45)

◆ Obliterated serial number on motor or parts (57)

◆ Altered VIN plate (71)

◆ Hair (34) & Fibres (25)

◆ Toolmark impressions (forced entry) (65)

◆ Paint (45)

◆ Punctured or slashed tires (63)

◆ Tools (66)

◆ Toolmark impressions (Cut wires) (65)

Miscellaneous:

◆ Fingerprints (27)

◆ Vehicle parts (70)

"L" Vehicle Collision

◆ Blood (5), Hair (34), Fibres (25), Fingerprints (27), Alcohol/Drugs (68)

◆ Footwear impressions (30)

◆ Tiremarks (62)

◆ Lights (38)

Miscellaneous:

Comparison standards from vehicle occupants to determine identity of driver.

"M" Provincial Coroners Act/Fatality Inquiries Act

Routine Autopsy Exhibits:

◆ Blood (5)

  – Cardiac blood

  – Peripheral blood

◆ Liver (39)

◆ Urine (69)

◆ Stomach contents (59)

◆ Vitreous humor (72)

Miscellaneous:

◆ Bile (4)

◆ Brain tissue (6)

◆ Cerebrospinal fluid (10)

◆ Flesh samples around wound (76)

◆ Lungs (41)

◆ Foreign objects (e.g. bullets, etc.)—see appropriate section

"N" Suspect

Sexual Assault/Homicide

◆ Blood (5), Urine (69), Breath samples (7) for alcohol/drug analysis

◆ Blood (5), Hair (34), & Fibres (25) from victim (see instructions—Sexual Assault Examination Kit)

◆ Known samples for DNA analysis (18)

◆ Lipstick/cosmetics from victim (15)

◆ Suspect's clothing (14)

◆ Weapons (74)

B & E/Vehicle Theft

◆ Known samples for DNA analysis (18), if applicable

◆ Outer clothing (14)

◆ Footwear (30)

◆ Visible glass (32), Paint (45), and/or Safe insulation (54)

◆ Tools (66)

Firearm Used

◆ Ammunition (3)

◆ Gunshot residue (33)

◆ Firearms (29)

Arson

◆ Outer clothing (14)

◆ Footwear (30)

◆ Matches (42)

Hit and Run

◆ Known samples for DNA analysis (18)

◆ Outer clothing if broken window involved (14)

"O" Prohibited Weapons (Chemical)

◆ Prohibited weapon (mace, tear gas) (52)

Miscellaneous:

◆ Submit intact container to Toxicology Section (52)

PART II: COLLECTION AND PRESERVATION OF EVIDENCE

1. Accelerants

(Lab Services Manual, App. 1-2, Sections 16 and 28)

◆ place in clean, unlined metal cans (unused, direct from supplier) or in Mason jars (do not invert rubber seals on lids of jars) or in nylon bags;

◆ if nylon bags are used as containers, submit one empty one (without opening) as a standard for comparison;

◆ cut up pieces of debris to make them fit into the containers;

◆ store in freezer until submitted to laboratory;

◆ package and ship separately from liquids and suspected accelerants;

◆ small glass bottles with teflon-lined screw caps are the preferred container for liquid accelerants. Metal cans may leak or corrode and Mason jars are more susceptible to breakage and leaking due to the interaction of the accelerant and their seals.

Comparison Standards:

◆ accelerant standards from scene or local neighbourhood should be packaged the same as unknown, suspected accelerants, but in separate containers.

2. Altered Documents

(Lab Services Manual, App. 1-2, Sec. 7)

◆ place altered documents in document protectors, plastic or paper envelopes.

Comparison Standards:

◆ collect any equipment/materials (typewriter, pen, paper, etc.) suspected of being used to alter the documents and place in exhibit envelopes.

2.A Travel Documents

(Lab Services Manual, App. 1-2, Sec. 41)

◆ if dealing with travel documents, contact the Central Forensic Laboratory at (613) 993-0664.

3. Ammunition

(Lab Services Manual, App. 1-2, Sec. 2)

◆ unload firearm, recover from scene, or seize from suspect;

◆ do not mark ammunition;

◆ ammunition components should be checked for other foreign materials, rinsed clean with water and dried;

◆ avoid altering or damaging ammunition during recovery and transit;

◆ wrap in soft material and place in containers which can be sealed and marked for identification;

◆ do not violate Transportation of Dangerous Goods Act when forwarding unfired ammunition to the Laboratory;

◆ bullets or bullet fragments can often be located by x-raying. Such equipment is often available at medical or veterinary facilities. Most Firearms sections have x-ray equipment for locating projectiles in small objects.

4. Bile

(Lab Services Manual, App. 1-2, Sec. 9)

◆ place in a vial and seal. Keep cool;

◆ to be collected if narcotics (e.g. morphine) are suspected.

5. Blood

Note: Blood exhibits are described under the following categories:

A. alcohol analysis

B. drug or poison analysis

C. DNA analysis of blood

D. blood stain pattern analysis

* All blood exhibits should be refrigerated until forwarded to the Laboratory (do not freeze). Ensure all vials are properly sealed and labelled.

5A. Alcohol Analysis

(Lab Services Manual, App. 1-2, Sec. 1)

Use Forensic Blood Collection Kit for all cases. If not available or if Kit vials have expired, then use two fresh 10 mL grey-stoppered vacuum tubes.

i)   suspect (driving offence)

   –   by demand if breath testing not possible;

   –   refer to instructions in Kit.

ii) suspect (non-driving offence) or victim

   –   by consent.

iii) deceased person

   –   obtain blood from femoral blood vessel or intact heart.

In all cases mix blood gently with vial contents.

5.B Drug or Poison Analysis

(Lab Services Manual, App. 1-2, Sec. 9)

i)   deceased person

   –   collect 8 grey-stoppered vacuum tubes of blood. Samples of both cardiac and peripheral blood should be included and labelled as such.

ii) suspect/victim

   –   collect 2 grey-stoppered vacuum tubes of blood.

iii) suspect—driving offence (by consent only)

   –   collect 2 grey-stoppered vacuum tubes of blood;

   –   collect 1 sample of urine in vacuum tube or lab-type suitable container.

   *   *If cocaine is suspected, one tube of blood should be collected in a grey-stoppered vacuum tube, refrigerated and submitted to the toxicology section without delay.*

Note: Grey-stoppered vacuum tubes contain a white powder, sodium fluoride, as a preservative.

5.C DNA Analysis of Blood

(Lab Services Manual, App. 1-2, Sec. 3)

i)   blood stains on absorbent material (e.g. carpet, clothing)

   –   *air dry the stains completely;*

   –   package each item separately.

ii) blood stains on other surfaces (e.g. walls, weapons)

   –   if item is large, such as a wall, cut out a portion and proceed as in (i), or;

    – *allow stain to air dry completely;*

    – scrape dried blood into a vial using a scalpel or other tool, or;

    – using water, moisten a small piece of cotton cloth or swab and, using tweezers, rub the stain until the cloth or swab are dark red. If more stain is present, repeat the process. Place in an appropriate container and air dry completely;

    – proceed as in (i).

  iii) liquid blood stains

    – soak up with clean cotton cloth or threads to obtain a dark red colour;

    – proceed as in (i).

Comparison Samples:

◆ one 10 mL mauve-stoppered vacuum tube (contains EDTA as an anticoagulant) of blood;

◆ refrigerate (do not freeze) until brought to the Laboratory.

  * *Blood samples must arrive at the Forensic Laboratory within 5 days. If this is not possible, make a stain of the blood on clean white cloth, dry the stain, place in a plastic bag and submit to Laboratory.*

5.D Blood Stain Pattern Analysis

◆ protect the scene;

◆ do not remove the body;

◆ any photographs taken should include close-ups of the stained areas;

◆ outside blood stains should be covered or photographed immediately;

◆ contact Regional Forensic Identification Support Section personnel at the Laboratory.

6. Brain Tissue

(Lab Services Manual, App. 1-2, Sec. 1)

◆ place in a leak-proof container. Keep refrigerated;

◆ to be collected if solvents (e.g. glue, PAM, cleaning fluids) are suspected.

7. Breath Samples (non-driving related offences)

(Lab Services Manual, App. 1-2, Sec. 1)

◆   by consent;

◆   have a proper Breath Test conducted obtaining two suitable samples of breath.

8. Building Products

(Lab Services Manual, App. 1-2, Sections 20, 26, 32 and 39)

◆   may be found on clothing, tools, cars, etc.;

◆   small particles may be submitted in plastic bags or vials.

Comparison Standards:

◆   standards should be from damaged areas;

◆   package separately in vials or bags.

9.   Buttons

(Lab Services Manual, App. 1-2, Sec. 14)

◆   package carefully to avoid loss of sewing threads or fibres adhering to the button.

Comparison Samples:

◆   clothing with missing buttons.

10. Cerebrospinal Fluid (CSF)

(Lab Services Manual, App. 1-2, Sec. 1)

◆   one vial from Forensic Blood Collection Kit or 10 mL grey-stoppered vacuum tube;

◆   seal stopper and label vial with appropriate markings;

◆   refrigerate (do not freeze) exhibits until conveyed to Laboratory.

11. Charred Documents

(Lab Services Manual, App. 1-2, Sec. 4)

◆   if located in a container which can be conveniently moved, carefully transport the entire container and contents in person to the Laboratory;

◆ if charred materials must be physically disturbed, carefully slip a sheet of paper or thin cardboard under the exhibits, place in a box lined with tissue and transport to the Laboratory in person.

12. Chequewriter Impressions

(Lab Services Manual, App. 1-2, Sec. 29)

◆ place cheques bearing suspected impressions in document protectors or plastic or paper envelopes;

◆ if at all possible, submit the chequewriter to the Laboratory for examination without making any adjustments or impressions;

◆ if it is not possible to submit the chequewriter, obtain several impressions at settings at which the machine was found;

◆ prepare five to ten specimen impressions of each dollar amount appearing on the questioned cheques, and then take samples of all numbers in all positions;

◆ if possible, vary the intensity of the impressions by exerting light to heavy pressure on the handle of the chequewriter.

13. Cigarette Butts

(Lab Services Manual, App. 1-2, Sec. 35)

◆ do not handle with bare hands;

◆ air dry the stains completely;

◆ package in separate containers.

Comparison Standards:

◆ submit cosmetic standards in plastic bags, vials, etc.

14. Clothing

14.A Presence of Hair, Fibres or Foreign Particles

(Lab Services Manual, App. 1-2, Sections 10, 14, 20, 22, 26, 32 and 39)

◆ sweep the floor where the suspect will undress;

◆ have each suspect stand on 2 clean sheets of paper when removing clothing (discard bottom sheet in contact with floor);

◆ submit folded paper separately (plastic evidence bags);

◆ air dry clothing taking care not to shake off any loosely attached particles;

◆ package each article of clothing separately in sealed evidence bags
   or clean paper bags and fold the top over several times before
   sealing;

◆ describe the location of any observed stains of interest on the
   accompanying Form C-414. *Do not mark stains;*

◆ indicate on the correspondence (C-414) whether the clothing/
   footwear is wet.

Comparison Samples:

◆ refer to Cosmetics (#15), DNA Analysis of Known Samples (#18),
   Fibres (#25), Glass (#32), Paint (#45), Safe Insulation (#54),
   Lubricants (#40).

14.B Arson Suspect's Clothing

(Lab Services Manual, App. 1-2, Sec. 16)

◆ place in clean unlined metal cans or Mason jars and freeze, if
   possible, until submitted to Laboratory;

◆ if articles of clothing are too large for cans or jars, pillow pack them
   in nylon evidence bags;

◆ call the section to get advice on packaging/shipping. If nylon bags
   are used as containers, submit at least one empty one (without
   opening) as a standard for comparison.

Comparison Standards:

◆ if plastic bags are used as containers, submit at least two (empty) as
   standards.

14.C Gunshot Residue (GSR) for Range Determination

(Lab Services Manual, App. 1-2, Sections 30 and 45)

◆ if wet, hang to dry at room temperature;

◆ protect the area near the bullet hole and other areas suspected of
   bearing GSR from further contamination;

◆ do not cover the bullet hole or suspect areas with other parts of the
   clothing;

◆ each item of clothing should be packed separately to prevent a
   transfer of residue;

◆ clothing should be packed in paper bags to prevent growth of mould.

14.D Blood, Semen, or Saliva Stains

(Lab Services Manual, App. 1-2, Sections 3 and 33)

◆   air dry any wet stains;

◆   package all clothing items separately.

15. Cosmetics (lipstick, eyeliner, etc.)

(Lab Services Manual, App. 1-2, Sec. 35)

◆   on the C-414, describe area of suspected cosmetic stains on clothing;

◆   submit clothing in clean paper bags with the tops folded over several times before sealing.

Comparison Standards:

◆   submit cosmetic standards in plastic bags, vials, etc.

16. Counterfeiting Exhibits

(Lab Services Manual, App. 1-2, Sec. 6)

Note: Counterfeits can include currency, security documents and travel documents. Refer to Travel documents (#2A) for submission of this evidence. Counterfeiting exhibits are described and categorized according to the main stages of printing production. The printing process most often used in counterfeiting activities is the "offset" method as illustrated in Scene "E". However, other printing processes may be employed, namely intaglio, letterpress and silk screen. Before conducting a printing plant search, investigators are encouraged to consult with counterfeit specialists at the Central Forensic Laboratory, (613) 993-0664, who are available to assist with the search.

    The presence of Laboratory personnel at the scene is beneficial to both the investigative unit and the Laboratory.

16.A Graphic Arts Photography (Scene E— process camera and darkroom)

This stage is needed to provide the necessary films (negatives) for plate-making. These exhibits can be found inside the process camera and in the darkroom.

i)   genuine documents

    –   initial and place in plastic envelope. Initials should be placed on the non-printed border area;

    –   submit to the Laboratory before sending to the Ident. Section for fingerprinting. Label accordingly.

ii)   artwork (pasteups, positives, blow-ups, line drawings, etc.)

-   place in plastic envelopes. Do not fold. Pasteups are subject to falling apart. Special care must be taken to ensure they remain intact.

iii)   negatives

-   secure in paper envelopes as undried film may stick to plastic protectors. Do not fold.

iv)   grey scale

-   very important in correlating a process camera to counterfeit. Initial the package separately.

16.B Stripping (Scene E—light table)

This operation is needed to assemble photographic films (negatives) for plate making.

 i)   flats (negatives mounted on sheets of coloured paper)

-   ensure arrangement of negatives remains intact.

ii)   artwork

-   do not fold.

16.C Plate Making (Scene E—plate burner)

Offset plates are produced by exposing a flat of films to the light-sensitive plate in close contact and under a strong light source. A plate burner (see illustration) is normally used. A carbon arc and a small vacuum frame occasionally replace the modern plate burner unit.

 i)   flats

-   same as (B.i) above.

ii)   plates

-   secure flat in paper envelopes. Do not clean ink from plates.

16.D Presswork (Scene E—press area)

Most parts of the offset printing press, upon which is highly valuable evidence, can easily be removed with tools found on the premises.

*   *Do not operate press under any circumstances.*

 i)   offset plate

-   remove from the plate cylinder and secure in a paper envelope. Initials should be placed in the non-image area;

      – do not remove ink anywhere;

      – used plates may be found elsewhere on the premises.

ii)   rubber blanket(s)

      – remove from the offset cylinder and place in a paper envelope.

Note: Impression may not be readily visible under normal lighting. Although the pertinent images may not be readily visible on the rubber blanket, they may be deciphered at the Laboratory. Used and stored rubber blankets may be found elsewhere on the premises. They may have strong evidential value.

iii) impression cylinder

      – often bears inked images of the counterfeit document. Close-up photographs of the impression cylinder should be taken if relevant evidence is found. Removing this cylinder is a complicated task which should be referred to a press mechanic.

iv) printed sheets

      – place in paper envelopes or in boxes and label accordingly.

v)   scraps of paper

      – refers to (#16.D.iv).

16.E Cutting and Trimming (Scene E—paper cutter and garbage)

The sheets of printed material are cut and trimmed with electric or manually operated guillotines. An office paper cutter may also be used. Stacks of counterfeits, whether completely or partially cut, should be preserved intact. Physical matches of paper and blade are often successful.

i)   uncut and partially cut sheets of paper

      – do not change the sequence of the sheets within a bundle. Place in a box and fill the vacant space to avoid disturbance of the striation patterns.

Comparison Standards:

      – use blank sheets of paper found on location and take samples from the guillotine blade. The following steps should be taken:

      a)   samples should be taken from:

            – the entire length of the blade;

            – both sides of the blade.

      b)   each bundle of paper should be identified as to originating from the front or back side of the blade.

ii) trimmings and partial impressions

   – same as above.

Comparison Standards:

   – same as above.

iii) guillotine blade(s)

   – record serial number and remove from guillotine once the comparison standard has been taken;

   – process other stored blades in the same manner.

   * *Mechanical guillotine should be operated by experienced person.*

16.F Garbage Cans

Valuable evidence is often recovered from garbage cans, both within the premises and outside.

 i) scraps of negatives, artwork, plates and paper

   – place in boxes and label accordingly;

   – ink analysis may prove valuable;

   – a complete list of all chemicals required in the processing of photographs, films, plates, etc. should be compiled. Their evidentiary value should be discussed with laboratory personnel.

17. Credit Cards

(Lab Services Manual, App. 1-2, Sec. 6)

◆ when dealing with altered or fabricated credit cards, consult with the Document Section and/or Central Bureau for Counterfeits at the Central Forensic Laboratory;

◆ forward all pertinent equipment seized to the Laboratory, e.g. embossing machines, encoders, tipping ribbons, etc.;

◆ attempt to obtain original copies of all suspect credit card invoices;

◆ place credit cards and invoices in separate document protectors or plastic or paper envelopes.

18. DNA Analysis of Known Samples

(Lab Services Manual, App. 1-2, Sections 22 and 33)

◆ collect known samples from all persons who might reasonably be expected to have contributed questioned stains or samples;

◆ collect both a known hair sample and a known buccal swab;

◆ known hair samples should consist of about 100 hairs (about 20 from each of five different areas of the scalp) collected by pulling and combing;

◆ known buccal swabs should be obtained by rubbing the inside of the cheek with a swab or dental rolls, or through use of a special buccal swab collection kit. Ensure that swabs are thoroughly air-dried before packaging.

19. Drug Paraphernalia

(Lab Services Manual, App. 1-2, Sections 8 and 9)

◆ syringes and other drug paraphernalia found at the scene should be submitted;

Note: Care must be taken with used needles, etc. which may bear contaminated blood (i.e. Hepatitis, AIDS);

 * *Caution: Non-biological liquids should be handled with care and placed in screw-capped glass containers, not allowed to invert. (Solvents and caustics can dissolve plastic containers and lids.)*

20. Drugs

(Lab Services Manual, App. 1-2, Sec. 9)

◆ place in a plastic vial.

Comparison Standards:

◆ secure any similar pills at crime scene ensuring that they are clearly segregated and identified from unknown pills.

21. Excise Exhibits

(Lab Services Manual, App. 1-2, Sec. 34)

Note: All excise exhibits should be refrigerated until forwarded to the Laboratory (Do Not Freeze). Ensure bottles are sealed with neck and safety labels (forms E-128A and E-128B) and initialled. Complete the body labels (form E-128) and attach to container so that serial number on the neck is visible.

21.A Distilled Product

◆ place in clean, dry polyethylene bottle;

◆ completely fill the container;

◆ submit at least 10-30 mL of sample.

21.B Mash and Wash

◆   place in a clean, dry polyethylene bottle;

◆   half fill the container to allow for gaseous expansion caused by fermentation processes. If possible, add a preservative (e.g. sodium bisulfate) to prevent further fermentation;

◆   submit at least 150 mL of sample. If sold particles (e.g. fruit, grain, etc.) are present, submit a representative quantity.

21.C Worm (i.e. liquid content)

◆   place in a clean dry polyethylene bottle;

◆   submit the complete sample.

22. Explosive Debris

(Lab Services Manual, App. 1-2, Sec. 12)

◆   contact the nearest Explosive Disposal Unit so that the scene can be searched for other bombs and devices;

◆   locate the seat of the blast and collect debris from this location;

◆   search outward from the seat of the blast in some systematic pattern and collect pieces of debris;

◆   place explosive debris in air-tight containers such as metal cans, mason jars and tamper-proof exhibit bags;

◆   remove any unexpended explosive substances from the debris and send it separately (refer to Explosive Substances (#24));

◆   be alert for metal fragments, tape fragments, pieces of wire, fragments of explosive wrappers (paper or plastic), clock mechanism parts, fuse, battery parts. Collect and package separately.

Comparison Standards:

◆   control samples and items from any suspect should be packaged and kept separate from scene samples and sent separately to the Laboratory.

23. Explosive Devices

(Lab Services Manual, App. 1-2, Sec. 12)

◆   contact the nearest Explosives Disposal Unit to render the device safe;

◆   device components (power sources, timing units, wires, blasting cap) may be handled by either CBDC or EDU;

◆ if unexpended explosive substance is found and laboratory analysis is required, refer to instructions under Explosive Substances (#24);

◆ preserve tape, paper, etc. for fingerprinting in metal cans or glass jars.

Comparison Standards:

◆ package and keep separate from questioned items;

◆ send separately to the Laboratory.

24. Explosive Substances

(Lab Services Manual, App. 1-2, Sec. 12)

◆ contact the nearest Explosives Disposal Unit for assistance in determining the stability of the explosive;

◆ send no more than 20 grams of each unexpended explosive to the Laboratory using the following procedure:

  – contact your nearest RCMP Forensic Laboratory to obtain the Explosive Transport Container (ETC) which is the *only approved shipping container* for unexpended explosive samples;

  – using the teflon vials provided with ETC, package the explosive in 10 gram quantities per vial and place in the ETC following the instructions provided;

  – nitroglycerine must be diluted 1:10 with methyl hydrate before submitting in the ETC;

  – complete the documentation exactly as indicated in instructions provided and ship to the designated Forensic Laboratory (see below) by courier or air;

  – contact the designated Laboratory by phone before shipping the ETC.

◆ Designated RCMP Forensic Laboratories:

  – east of the Manitoba/Saskatchewan border: send to RCMP Central Forensic Laboratory in Ottawa;

  – west of the Manitoba/Saskatchewan border: send to RCMP Forensic Laboratory in [location missing in original]

Comparison Standards:

◆ package and keep separate from scene samples;

◆ send separately to the Laboratory;

◆ if unexpended explosives are involved, an ETC must be used for shipping.

25. Fibres

(Lab Services Manual, App. 1-2, Sec. 14)

◆ if on movable object or garment, package the item;

◆ if item cannot be submitted, then remove fibres with fingers or tweezers;

◆ place fibres in vial or other secure container;

◆ seal and label container;

◆ alternatively, fibres may be removed by taping the surface with clear transparent tape;

◆ place the tape, sticky side down, on plastic sheets and label;

◆ do not use tape to remove fibres if foreign paint chips/smears are also to be compared to known standards. The tape precludes a meaningful physical or chemical comparison of the paint fragments.

Comparison Samples:

◆ collect samples of items which may have transferred fibres, e.g. clothing, rugs, blankets;

◆ package carefully and individually to avoid contamination of other exhibits.

26. Fingernail Scrapings/Clippings

(Lab Services Manual, App. 1-2, Sections 3 and 14)

◆ are of limited forensic value;

◆ collect only if blood and/or other material is visible;

◆ collect using a fingernail clipper, toothpick or other such tool;

◆ refrigerate until exhibits can be brought to the Laboratory.

Comparison Samples:

◆ blood/saliva standard from accused;

◆ clothing from suspect.

27. Fingerprints

◆ submit all paper exhibits to the Laboratory for examination before processing for fingerprints;

◆ place paper exhibits for fingerprinting in documents protectors, plastic, or paper envelopes and clearly mark each envelope *"Fingerprints—Do Not Touch"* on the outside and make a note on the Request for Analysis (form C-414) as well.

28. Fire Debris

(Lab Services Manual, App. 1-2, Sec. 16)

◆ place in clean, unlined metal cans (unused, direct from supplier, store with lids on), in Mason jars (do not invert rubber seals on lids of jars) or in heat-sealed nylon bags specially designed for fire debris (e.g. special RCMP exhibit bags (check label), nylon bags or other plastic bags designed for fire debris);

◆ leave 1"-2" space at top of can free of debris;

◆ if ordinary plastic bags must be used, double bag;

◆ if plastic bags are used, seal well. Special plastic bags may be heat-sealed. Otherwise fold over several times and seal with the label portion or tape;

◆ if nylon bags are used as containers, submit one empty one (without opening) as a standard for comparison;

◆ cut up large pieces of debris and fill container one-half to two-thirds with debris;

◆ do not dry exhibits before packaging;

◆ store in freezer until submitted to the Laboratory;

◆ package and ship separately from liquids and suspected accelerants.

Comparison Standards:

◆ refer to Accelerants (#1);

◆ same type of material as questioned debris, sampled from where no accelerant is suspected of being used;

◆ package in similar fashion as suspected material, but in separate containers;

◆ retain comparison standards of substrate materials until the lab requests them.

29. Firearms

(Lab Services Manual, App. 1-2, Sec. 15)

◆ unload and affix proper identification tags;

◆ do not disassemble a firearm unless absolutely necessary, particularly if its mechanical operating condition is pertinent to the investigation;

◆ if recovered from water or in an excessively soiled condition, contact the Firearms Section at the Laboratory for cleaning and preservation procedures;

◆   ensure that firearms are transported in accordance with the Prohibited Weapons Control Regulations; Restricted Weapons and Firearms Control Regulations; Storage, Display, Handling and Transportation of Certain Firearms Regulations and other relevant Federal or Provincial Acts.

30. Footwear

(Lab Services Manual, App. 1-2, Sec. 18)

◆   collect shoes and other types of footwear;

◆   ensure that the items are dry;

◆   collect items with impressions i.e. brake pedal, wood, paper, etc.;

◆   contact nearest Identification Section.

31. Gambling Devices (Cards, Dice, etc.)

(Lab Services Manual, App. 1-2, Sec. 7)

◆   card packages should be submitted in their original condition. *Do not open sealed packages*;

◆   do not combine gambling materials into a common package. Separate them according to where they were found;

◆   submit any wrapping materials found in waste baskets or on the floor;

◆   include any materials (dye solutions, solvents, etc.) believed to be used for marking playing cards;

◆   keep dice together as pairs where possible.

32. Glass

(Lab Services Manual, App. 1-2, Sec. 20)

◆   package in leak-proof plastic vials;

◆   carefully mark where sample was taken from on the container;

◆   large chips or fragments of glass should be double-wrapped;

◆   protect outer edges if physical matching is believed possible.

Comparison Standards:

◆   package in leak-proof plastic vials;

◆   package separately from questioned exhibits;

◆   take glass sample from each pane of glass broken, package separately and clearly indicate its source;

◆   take a control glass sample from the frame of each pane of broken glass, label as to source and package separately.

33. Gunshot Residue

(Lab Services Manual, App. 1-2, Sections 30 and 45)

◆ if sampling the hands and face of a suspect, follow instructions in Gunshot Residue Kit, if available. If not available, contact your Laboratory regarding gunshot residue analysis;

◆ if hand and face samples cannot be taken, consider submitting the exterior clothing of the suspect. Each item of clothing should be packaged separately in paper bags. Refer to Clothing (#14C).

34. Hair

(Lab Services Manual, App. 1-2, Sec. 22)

34.A Human Hair

◆ if on movable object or garment, package the item;

◆ if on a stationary item, remove hairs with fingertips or tweezers, or by applying clear cellulose tape (e.g. Scotch) to the area in question;

◆ place loose hairs in a vial or other secure container;

◆ seal and label container.

Comparison Samples:

◆ collect known hair samples from all persons who might reasonably be expected to have contributed questioned hairs;

◆ *do not cut hair;*

◆ Scalp: comb first and then pull hairs from five different areas of the scalp, collecting a total of about 100 hairs;

◆ Pubic: comb first and then pull hairs, collecting 30-50 in total. Package combed and pulled hairs separately;

◆ Other body areas: pull about 30 hairs from the area of interest, e.g. limb, chest, beard.

34.B Animal Hair

◆ As #34A above.

Comparison Samples:

◆ when possible, collect standard sample from the animal involved;

◆ take hair from various areas of the animal involved, being sure to include the range of colours and lengths present.

35. Handwriting/Handprinting

(Lab Services Manual, App. 1-2, Sec. 23)

◆ place documents in document protectors, plastic or paper envelopes;

◆ keep questioned and known exhibits separate. Segregate samples collected from different suspect writers, clearly identifying each group;

◆ ensure that the originals of documents are submitted whenever possible;

◆ if documents are to be checked for fingerprints, send exhibits to Laboratory first, making note on Request For Analysis (form C414) that the exhibits are to be subsequently checked for prints.

Comparison Standards:

◆ obtain "collected" and "requested" specimens from all suspect writers;

◆ *"Collected"* samples are those whose authorship can be proven and which were completed without knowledge that they would be used for comparison purposes. These samples should contain letters and letter combinations found in the questioned text;

◆ *"Requested"* samples are those which are prepared at the request of the investigator and require the duplication of all conditions surrounding the production of the questioned document (e.g. exact wording of the questioned text, type of paper/document, writing instrument, etc.). These specimens should be dictated by the investigator without the writer viewing the questioned documents;

◆ for questioned signatures, "requested" samples should consist of 15-20 repetitions of the signature written on separate pieces of paper similar in form to the questioned exhibit;

◆ for extended questioned writings, such as anonymous or threatening letters, "requested" samples require 2-3 repetitions of the entire letter.

36. Indentations on Paper

(Lab Services Manual, App. 1-2, Sec. 7)

◆ place documents suspected of bearing indentations in document protectors, or in envelopes, between thin sheets of cardboard to preserve and protect any latent impressions;

◆ ensure that extraneous indentations are not introduced when initialling exhibits or labelling the package if mailing to the Laboratory;

◆ do not treat for fingerprints until examined by the Document Section.

37. Ink

(Lab Services Manual, App. 1-2, Sec. 24)

◆ various typewriter ribbon, stamp pad and writing inks can be differentiated by analysis;

◆ place documents bearing the contested ink impressions in protective paper envelopes and package any suspected instruments separately.

38. Lights

(Lab Services Manual, App. 1-2, Sec. 19)

◆ protection of light/lamp filaments is imperative;

◆ if a lamp is broken, protect filament and posts with a styrofoam cup taped in place;

◆ if the lamp is not broken, wrap carefully and submit;

◆ if filaments are not present on post, check scene for them. If found, pack carefully and submit;

Note: Do not test lamp at scene.

39. Liver

(Lab Services Manual, App. 1-2, Sec. 9)

◆ obtain approximately 100 grams of liver tissue and place in a leak-proof container. Keep cool.

40. Lubricants, Sexual Assault

(Lab Services Manual, App. 1-2, Sec. 35)

◆ on Form C-414 describe the areas of observed staining on undergarments of the victim and submit in a plastic bag;

◆ if obvious on a vaginal swab, submit using a glass vial or test tube.

Comparison Standards:

◆ possible standards taken from suspect's property (e.g. vaseline, cosmetics, hand creams, cooking oils, etc.);

◆ submit in original containers.

41. Lungs

(Lab Services Manual, App. 1-2, Sec. 1)

◆ place in a leak-proof and air-tight container. Keep cool;

◆ to be collected if solvents (e.g. glue, PAM, cleaning fluids) are suspected.

42. Matches, Paper

(Lab Services Manual, App. 1-2, Sec. 19)

◆ carefully wrap torn/burnt paper matches in tissue paper and place each match in its own individual protective container (i.e. vial or reinforced envelope);

◆ take care not to break burnt matches and, if broken, include all match pieces in the same container.

Comparison Standards:

◆ obtain and package separately all match booklets from the suspects.

43. Meat

(Lab Services Manual, App. 1-2, Sec. 17)

◆ for identification of animal source, contact your regional Laboratory for referral to an examining laboratory;

◆ if poisoning is suspected, contact the Toxicology Section at your regional Laboratory.

44. Medications/Chemicals

(Lab Services Manual, App. 1-2, Sec. 9)

◆ submit a list of such items available at the place of death including prescriptions, "over the counter" medications and chemicals, herbicides and insecticides.

45. Paint

(Lab Services Manual, App. 1-2, Sec. 26)

◆ take paint samples from damaged areas of vehicles, buildings (e.g. door frame), fences, posts, safes, etc.;

◆ submit parts of damaged material if possible, especially if smearing is present (e.g. bumper extensions, parts of door frames);

◆ remove each paint sample with a clean scalpel blade, being careful to obtain all layers of paint present;

◆ do not use adhesive tape for lifting paint unless necessary;

◆ package in folded paper inside a sealed envelope (contact lab for instructions on packaging), metal canisters or plastic vials with snap-on lids;

◆ submit liquid paint samples in paint tins or place on a glass slide, dry and submit (liquid samples must be shipped in accordance with the Transportation of Dangerous Goods Act);

◆ protect edges if physical matching is desired;

◆ lifting foreign paint with tape is unacceptable in all circumstances;

◆ leakproof plastic bags should only be used as a last resort.

Comparison Standards:

◆ take paint standards from damaged areas of vehicles, doors, etc.;

◆ submit liquid paint samples in paint tins or place paint on a glass slide, dry and submit (liquid samples must be submitted in accordance with the Transportation of Dangerous Goods Act);

◆ package standards separately from unknown paint samples to avoid cross contamination;

◆ sample and package each sample separately taking care to avoid contamination with each other or with unknown/foreign paint samples.

46. Paper

(Lab Services Manual, App. 1-2, Sec. 27)

◆ carefully segregate questioned and specimen papers;

◆ place each suspect document in a document protector, plastic, or paper envelope.

Comparison Standards:

◆ obtain samples from each source and package separately.

47. Photocopiers/Photocopies

(Lab Services Manual, App. 1-2, Sec. 5)

◆ ensure that photocopied documents are placed in paper envelopes rather than plastic protectors to prevent the toner on the photocopy from sticking to the plastic.

Comparison Standards:

◆ when taking photocopier standards, do not clean the platen glass or adjust any components of the machine;

◆ obtain 10 samples from the machine with the lid closed and no original document in the copier;

◆ place a clean sheet of legal size paper on the platen glass and obtain an additional 5 samples from the copier;

◆   place a clean sheet of graph paper on the platen glass and obtain an additional 5 samples from the copier;

◆   submit all samples in addition to the original blank sheet and the piece of graph paper;

◆   determine if a maintenance contract exists for the copier and obtain copies of any adjustments made to the machine for the period in question.

48. Physical Match

(Lab Services Manual, App. 1-2, Sec. 19)

◆   collect all torn paper, tape, foil products and place in protective containers;

◆   if paper are water-soaked or blood-stained, do not attempt to separate them but place them in a ventilated area to dry;

◆   do not attempt to remove, separate or straighten adhesive tape used;

◆   package torn items carefully to protect fragile torn edges.

Comparison Standards:

◆   submit the entire roll of tape from which the questioned tapes were suspected of being removed;

◆   include the entire pad of paper, receipt/cheque book or other materials believed to be the source of the questioned item(s);

◆   clearly identify all exhibits so as to maintain the continuity of the source of exhibits.

49. Plastic Bags

(Lab Services Manual, App. 1-2, Sec. 43)

◆   contact FL Regina or Halifax Chemistry Section;

◆   submit individual bags and portions of bags;

◆   avoid stretching;

◆   label carefully.

Comparison Samples:

◆   any opened packages or rolls and any individual bags or portions of bags.

Note: For other plastic comparisons not covered in this section or section 43, consult your regional laboratory's Chemistry Section.

50. Price Markers/Labellers

(Lab Services Manual, App. 1-2, Sec. 29)

◆ whenever possible, submit the price marker or labelling device to the Laboratory without operating or changing the device;

◆ forward any applicable rolls or refills of labels.

Comparison Standards:

◆ if it is impossible to submit the machine, make 10-20 specimens of each amount in question, including all digits/characters in the appropriate columns.

51. Printers (Computer)

(Lab Services Manual, App. 1-2, Sec. 29)

◆ whenever possible, submit the suspect computer printer to the Laboratory without operating or making any changes;

◆ if it is impossible to submit the machine, change the ribbon and generate two self-tests to produce samples of the resident type fonts;

◆ include the printer ribbon if impressions of the questioned printed text may remain on the ribbon;

◆ obtain, if possible, samples of correspondence from files which were executed with the same equipment on or about the date of the questioned document;

◆ if the printer has interchangeable type elements, prepare samples with each suspected element and include all type elements with the submission;

◆ if possible, use the printer and connected word processing equipment to prepare five specimens of the questioned text;

◆ label all specimens so produced with the name, serial number and location of the printer, and place them in document protectors, plastic, or paper envelopes.

52. Prohibited Weapons (Chemical)

(Lab Services Manual, App. 1-2, Sec. 9)

◆ offending chemical agents, e.g. tear gas, mace. The container should be submitted intact to the Toxicology section if identification of the active chemical constituents is required.

53. Rubber Stamps

(Lab Services Manual, App. 1-2, Sec. 29)

◆ place document bearing the questioned rubber stamp impression in a document protector, plastic, or paper envelope;

◆ wrap in separate containers all stamps and the stamp pads suspected of being used to produce the questioned impression;

◆ "date" stamps and "make your own" stamps should not be altered or changed in any way.

54. Safe Insulation

(Lab Services Manual, App. 1-2, Sec. 32)

◆ refer to Clothing (#14) and Tools (#66);

◆ particles of safe packing should be placed in leak-proof vials or bags;

◆ keep separate from clothing or tools.

Comparison Standards:

◆ remove sample of safe packing from each damaged area of the safe;

◆ package in leak-proof vials or plastic bags.

55. Saliva

(Lab Services Manual, App. 1-2, Sec. 33)

◆ air dry the stains completely;

◆ package each item separately;

◆ exhibits can be left at room temperature until taken to Laboratory.

Comparison Samples:

◆ see DNA Analysis of Known Samples (#18).

56. Semen

(Lab Services Manual, App. 1-2, Sec. 33)

◆ use RCMP Sexual Assault Examination Kit or equivalent if available, or;

◆ take one swab from each appropriate area of the victim (i.e. anal and oral swabs are not necessary when the sexual assault is vaginal only);

◆ include a vaginal wash where appropriate;

◆ *air dry the stains and swabs completely;*

◆ package each item separately;

◆ exhibits where blood is not involved can be left at room temperature until taken to Laboratory.

Comparison Samples:

◆ see DNA Analysis of Known Samples (#18).

57. Serial Number Obliterations

(Lab Services Manual, App. 1-2, Sec. 11)

◆ contact Firearms Section if item is difficult to transport to Laboratory.

58. Soil

(Lab Services Manual, App. 1-2, Sec. 10)

◆ place in clean, lined metal cans or in Mason jars (do not invert rubber seals on lids of jars);

◆ freeze if possible until submitted to the Laboratory.

Comparison Standards:

◆ refer to Accelerants (#1);

◆ soil sample from each area where no accelerant is suspected of being used.

59. Stomach Contents

(Lab Services Manual, App. 1-2, Sec. 9)

◆ collect some of the stomach contents in a leak proof container. Keep cool.

60. Suspect's Belongings

◆ clothing—refer to Clothing (#14);

◆ most items that would belong to a suspect can probably be packaged in leakproof evidence bags or folded and sealed paper bags (e.g. comb, etc.).

61. Tape (physical matching)

(Lab Services Manual, App. 1-2, Sec. 19)

◆   carefully package ensuring ends of tape are protected.

Comparison Standards:

◆   secure all partial rolls and pieces;

◆   protect ends.

62. Tiremarks

◆   contact nearest Identification Section.

63. Tires—Punctured or Slashed

(Lab Services Manual, App. 1-2, Sec. 36)

◆   it is not necessary to submit the entire tire. Cut an area around the puncture or slash.

64. Tissue (small fragments to be identified as human)

(Lab Services Manual, App. 1-2, Sections 3 and 33)

◆   place in a vial;

◆   freeze and keep in this condition until brought to Laboratory.

65. Tool Marks

(Lab Services Manual, App. 1-2, Sections 37 and 38)

◆   apply a protective covering to all areas in question;

◆   protect tool marks from damage or corrosion;

◆   the actual object bearing the tool mark or impression should be submitted when possible;

◆   if the tool mark cannot be removed, contact the nearest laboratory for advice on making casts of the tool mark;

◆   when the above is not feasible, remove portions of the exhibit containing the tool marks;

◆   keep tool mark impressions isolated from the suspect tools.

66. Tools

(Lab Services Manual, App. 1-2, Sec. 37)

◆ if damp, gently wipe moisture from tools with a soft cloth or paper towel. Do not allow to rust. Take care not to dislodge paint, glass or other foreign material that may be useful for chemical analysis;

◆ package carefully the ends of tools where foreign materials may be impacted;

◆ use plastic bags or styrofoam cups taped over the end to prevent further damage to the tools;

◆ send tools in a tightly-packed box to prevent movement;

◆ keep tools isolated from suspect tool marks.

Comparison Standards:

◆ refers to Glass (#32), Paint (#45), Safe Insulation (#54), Tool Marks (#65).

67. Typewriting

(Lab Services Manual, App. 1-2, Sec. 40)

◆ whenever possible submit the typewriter to the Laboratory;

◆ do not alter, adjust or type on the typewriter;

◆ ensure that the ribbon and all available type elements (printwheels, typeballs) are submitted for examination.

Comparison Standards:

◆ if it is impossible to submit the typewriter, before preparing any specimens remove any single-strike ribbon and replace it with another;

◆ one complete set of "direct carbon impressions" should be prepared with the typewriter by using a sheet of carbon paper with the typewriter in the "stencil" position;

◆ each character on the keyboard (upper and lower case) should be struck 5 times (vary the pressure of these impressions from light to heavy if the machine is a manual typewriter);

◆ additional specimens should be obtained by typing the entire questioned text several times using all suspected type elements;

◆ ensure that samples are taken using all available type elements (typeballs and printwheels), and that each sample is clearly identified as to the make, model, serial number, and style of type used.

68. Unknown Liquid or Powder (for alcohol, drug or poison analysis)

(Lab Services Manual, App. 1-2, Sections 1 and 9)

◆   submit in original container if possible;

◆   seal all liquid samples adequately to prevent evaporation or leakage;

◆   label container with appropriate markings.

69. Urine

(Lab Services Manual, App. 1-2, Sections 1 and 9)

Note: All urine exhibits should be refrigerated until forwarded to Laboratory (do not freeze). Ensure all vials are properly sealed and labelled.
Urine exhibits are described under the following categories:

A.   alcohol analysis

  i)   deceased person

  ii) suspect or victim

B.   drug/poison analysis

69.A Alcohol Analysis

i)   deceased person

–   one vial from Forensic Blood Collection Kit or 10 mL grey-stoppered vacuum tube.

ii) suspect or victim

–   only if blood sample cannot be obtained by consent;

–   if possible, collect two separate samples at one-half hour intervals. Note times of collection;

–   use a clean, dry urine specimen jar for each sample;

–   transfer a portion of each sample into separate Kit vial or vacuum tube.

In all cases mix urine gently with vial contents.

69.B Drug/Poison Analysis

◆   all available urine should be collected in red-stoppered vacutainer vials or plastic urine specimen jars.

70. Vehicle Parts

(Lab Services Manual, App. 1-2, Sec. 19 and 43)

◆ protect broken ends of moulding, aerials, trim, etc. that could be useful in physical matching;

◆ package in a plastic bag, etc.;

◆ box should be tightly packed to avoid movement of items.

Comparison Standards:

◆ package same as unknowns but do not allow contact between unknowns and comparison standards;

◆ if necessary, ship separately to the Laboratory.

71. VIN Plates (altered)

(Lab Services Manual, App. 1-2, Sec. 11)

◆ forward to Laboratory.

72. Vitreous Humor (for alcohol analysis)

(Lab Services Manual, App. 1-2, Sec. 1)

◆ one vial from Forensic Blood Collection Kit or 10 mL grey-stoppered vacuum tube;

◆ seal stopper and label vial with appropriate markings;

◆ refrigerate (do not freeze) exhibits until conveyed to Laboratory.

73. Water-Soaked Documents

(Lab Services Manual, App. 1-2, Sec. 7)

◆ whenever possible submit the documents personally to the Laboratory;

◆ if it is impossible to submit personally, air-dry documents prior to carefully packaging for mailing;

Note: Wet documents left in sealed plastic bags will promote mould growth;

◆ do not try to separate pages that are stuck together.

74. Weapons (for presence of hair or fibres)

(Lab Services Manual, App. 1-2, Sections 14 and 22)

◆ wrap carefully to ensure that no evidence is lost;

◆ submit for fibre search prior to fingerprinting;

◆ indicate that fingerprinting is required and the item will be handled accordingly.

Comparison Standards:

◆ any clothing items the weapon may have come in contact with. In the case of a head injury, hair standards will be necessary.

75. Wire (Tool mark examinations)

(Lab Services Manual, App. 1-2, Sec. 38)

◆ mark the end that you cut;

◆ the suspect end is left unmarked but covered with loose protective packing;

◆ do not cover the suspect end with tape.

76. Wounds (Gunshot residue)

(Lab Services Manual, App. 1-2, Sec. 30 and 45)

◆ obtain as large a sample as possible from around wound and do not clean;

◆ pin out on a flat surface (wood, cardboard, etc.) and place in a glass or plastic container;

◆ keep cool while transporting to the Laboratory or freeze should there be any delay in delivery;

◆ do not immerse in liquid preservatives.

TELEPHONE NUMBERS

Laboratory Location: _____

Laboratory Manager: _____

Administration Section: _____

Alcohol Section: _____

Biology Section: _____

Chemistry Section: _____

Documents Section: _____

Firearms Section: _____

Toxicology Section: _____

Identification Section: _____

CANADIAN CATALOGUING IN PUBLICATION DATA

Main entry under title :
Investigator's guide to forensic evidence

2nd ed.
Issued also in French under title:
Guide de collecte des éléments de preuve.
ISBN 0-662-23701-3
Cat. no. JS62-64/1995E

1. Evidence, Criminal – Handbooks, manuals, etc.
2. Crime scene searches – Handbooks, manuals, etc.
3. Criminal investigation – Handbooks, manuals, etc.
I. Royal Canadian Mounted Police.
   Forensic Laboratory services

HV8073.158 1995   363.2'52   C95-980224–X

PAID.393
Published by the Royal Canadian Mounted Police
Public Affairs and Information Directorate
for the Forensic Laboratory Services
© Minister of Supply and Services, Canada (1995)

Également disponible en français sous le titre
Guide de collecte des éléments de preuve.

Glossary of Terms

accused a suspect who has been charged with a crime

admissibility the likelihood of a piece of evidence to be allowed (by the judge) to be presented in a court case

admissions acts or words of a party offered as evidence against that party

adverse witness a witness called in support of one's own side, but whose evidence turns out to be unfavourable

affiant a person who makes and swears an affidavit

affidavit a written and witnessed statement of evidence that the maker swears and signs as proof of its truth

agent provocateur an informer or agent of the police who seeks to provoke a suspect into committing a crime

arrest detention of a citizen by a police officer combined with an intent to immediately take that person into police custody

asphyxia marked and potentially fatal deprivation of oxygen flow to body tissues (including the brain), usually due to a breathing obstruction

autopsy an examination of a dead body made to determine such issues as the cause and time of death; a post mortem examination

best evidence rule a legal rule requiring that wherever possible, the original document (the best evidence), rather than a reproduction, should be introduced in evidence

burden of proof the requirement of proving a particular fact or argument; the onus

case to meet usually, the sum of the prosecution's evidence (which dictates the evidence necessary to mount a supportable defence)

cautioning giving a suspect formal notice of his or her right to freedom from self-incrimination before questioning begins; "reading him his rights"

cavity search a search of the internal body cavities (mouth, vagina, etc.) of a suspect

charging the jury the judge's instructions to the jury, usually at the end of a trial, in preparation for the jury's deliberations

circumstantial evidence   evidence that logically supports a fact, but that is at least partly dependent on speculation

"clean" evidence   physical evidence that is free of taint related to mishandling by investigators or prosecutors

compellability   being without legal excuse (such as status as the accused's spouse) for not testifying

competence   being legally permitted to testify (based on the absence of factors such as age under 14 years or mental handicap)

confession   a voluntary statement by an accused, to a person in authority, that is intended to incriminate the accused

consciousness of guilt   a state of mind that (some believe) is capable of proof and that may support the actual guilt of the person experiencing it

consent search   a warrantless search that has been expressly permitted by the person (or the person in control of the private property) being searched

continuity   in the context of physical evidence, an ability to account for the whereabouts of the evidence (and the identity of those who have had access to it) from the time of its collection to the time it is entered as an exhibit in the trial record

corroborative evidence   independently sourced evidence that supports another piece of evidence

counselling records   notes and records made in the course of providing counselling services to a client/patient

crime scene   the location where a crime has been or is suspected to have been committed

crime scene core   the immediate location of the crime

crime scene perimeter   the area surrounding the crime scene core and including potential routes to and from the core

cross-examination   questioning a witness for the opposing side of the case

demonstrative evidence   evidentiary "tools" produced by a party to help explain a case, such as maps or photographs of the crime scene

deoxyribonucleic acid (DNA)   a biological compound that forms cell chromosomes and from which genetic information can be gleaned

detention short of arrest/investigative detention   the restraint of a person by a police officer (in the absence of an arrest), usually for the purpose of questioning

direct evidence   evidence that proves an important fact without the need to speculate

disclosure   a duty to show one's own evidence to the opposing party in a case

DNA warrant a specialized warrant permitting the collection of DNA evidence from the body of a suspect

documentary evidence a class of physical/real evidence that consists of documents of any kind, handwritten or mechanically produced

duty notes an officer's written record of the details of his or her attendance at a crime scene, an arrest, or a field investigation

evidence any information or physical material relied upon in legal proceedings to prove or disprove a fact or legal argument

ex parte (Latin) a legal proceeding decided in the absence of one of the parties likely to be affected by its result is said to be *ex parte*

examination-in-chief a party's questioning of its own witnesses

exculpatory statement a statement denying guilt made by the accused

exhibit any piece of evidence (real, demonstrative, or documentary) other than oral testimony that is "entered" in the trial record

exhibit report a standard form document that accompanies a piece of physical evidence and provides a description of the item and a record of any changes in its custody (such as out to a pathology lab and back) prior to trial

exigent circumstances urgent and pressing circumstances (that may justify a warrantless search)

forensics a discipline based on the collection and study of scientific information that is destined for use in legal proceedings

general warrant a court-sanctioned grant of permission to search a stipulated location for the purpose of collecting evidence

gunshot residue (GSR) trace substances left on surfaces (including the hand of the shooter) after the discharge of a firearm

handwash test a procedure in current use for the collection of gunshot residue evidence; it involves a suspect washing his or her hands in a substance containing chemical reagents

"having a view/look-see" an excursion by the judge and/or jury to a site outside the courtroom to view evidence that cannot reasonably be presented in court

hearsay evidence that is indirect in that it is being given by a witness who has heard it from another source; second-hand evidence

homicide team/squad a team of police officers with special training in the investigation of homicide and suspicious death

hydrodynamics the movement properties of water/liquids

identification officer police officer with special training in the analysis of physical evidence

independent recollection   a recollection of events being recounted in testimony that is separate from what can be gleaned from reading one's notes about those events

indictment   a form, often prepared after a fuller investigation, setting out the offence(s) on which a conviction will be sought at trial

inducements   promises, favours, threats, or representations made to the accused that may be perceived as efforts to coerce the accused into making a confession

information   a form, prepared at the time of the laying of a charge, describing the offence(s) with which a suspect has been charged

intent   sometimes called *mens rea*; the mental element of an offence that must be proved to secure a conviction

known standards/standards for comparison   samples of evidence (of the same type) collected or prepared for the purpose of analytical comparison with the evidence to be used at trial; control samples

latent evidence   evidence that must be collected or interpreted with the assistance of special technology, such as the application of a chemical reagent

latent fingerprint   a fingerprint that is not easily observed by the naked eye and that must be collected through scientific means

lay witness   any witness testifying about a subject matter in which he or she is not an expert

leading question   a question the phrasing of which "suggests" the answer sought

materiality   the degree to which a piece of evidence is necessary in proving a proposition

oath   a promise to tell the truth that is "sworn" with a hand on the Bible

oath helping   when one witness (improperly) expresses an opinion about the credibility of another witness

objection   a request that evidence about to be given be ruled inadmissible (by the judge)

oral testimony/*viva voce* evidence   the spoken (verbal) evidence of a witness as given under oath or affirmation in a legal proceeding

paraffin test   an obsolete test/collection method for gunshot residue

pathologist   a scientist/doctor specializing in the study of the causes of disease and death

perimeter search   usually, a search that consists of observations of a piece of private property made without physical intrusion on that property

perjury   lying while under oath or affirmation

person in authority a person who is involved in the prosecution of the accused, and whom the accused perceives as having authority over the course of the prosecution

plain view doctrine an accepted legal rule that prohibits warrantless searches unless the searching officer has first discovered illegal evidence in plain view

police informant privilege a privilege that attaches, in some situations, to the identity of a police informer, such as the provider of a "Crime Stoppers" tip

post mortem examination an examination of a dead body made to determine such issues as the cause and time of death; an autopsy

post mortem lividity a discolouration of certain parts of the body after death due to pooling of blood after circulation has ceased

prejudice the undesirable "side effects" of a piece of (usually, inflammatory) evidence that may be deemed unfair to the accused

preliminary hearing a hearing held before the real trial to determine preliminary issues, such as whether there is enough evidence to proceed to trial

***prima facie* evidence** evidence that is reliable on first impression, and that is accepted in the absence of any challenge to its validity

prior inconsistent statements statements made prior to trial that are inconsistent with statements made at trial

privilege a kind of protection (exemption from admissibility) that attaches to evidence produced in special circumstances, such as in the course of certain classes of relationships

privilege against self-incrimination a privilege exempting the accused from the obligation to give self-incriminating evidence (or any evidence at all)

probative value the relative relevance and materiality ("proof power") of a particular piece of evidence

proof beyond a reasonable doubt proof that is convincing beyond any doubt that a reasonable person could formulate

proof on a balance of probabilities proof that leaves the trier of fact at least 51 percent certain of the truth of a fact

propensity evidence evidence that is tendered to prove the "propensity" of an accused to act in a particular way

public interest and unity privilege a class of privilege protecting information the disclosure of which would threaten the public interest, such as, in some cases, the identity of undercover investigators

re-examination/re-direct a party's questioning of its own witnesses after cross-examination has been completed

real evidence physical objects (including documents in some cases) with a direct link to the crime that are introduced as evidence

relevance the tendency of a piece of evidence to prove or disprove a proposition

rigor mortis a temporary stiffening of the body after death due to an enzymatic reaction

scanning electron microscopy (SEM) test a newer method of interpreting gunshot residue evidence that requires a collection method less cumbersome than the chemical handwash

search incident to arrest a warrantless personal search that is permitted at the time of arrest

secondary documentary evidence a piece of documentary evidence that is other than an original, such as a photocopy

securing the crime scene a group of tasks that must be carried out by an officer arriving at a crime scene, including protecting from disturbance any potential evidence, and controlling access by other parties

similar fact evidence evidence that suggests that the accused has acted in the past in a way that is similar to the acts alleged as part of the offence being tried

solemn affirmation a promise to tell the truth without a hand on the Bible—for the non-religious—as provided for in s. 14 of the *Canada Evidence Act*

solicitor–client privilege an exemption from disclosure requirements for certain communications between a lawyer and client

spousal privilege an exemption from disclosure and compellability for the spouse of an accused

standard of proof the degree of certainty of the truth of a fact required before that fact can be relied on in support of a particular verdict or legal decision

statements against interest statements made by a person that seem to acknowledge guilt, a debt, etc.—the opposite of self-serving statements

subpoena a formal request, enforceable by the court, for a person's attendance in court to give testimony

telewarrant a warrant obtained through an expedited process over the telephone

trace elements chemical/biological substances in tiny quantities

transference an imprint or trace left on one surface or object by another

trial record the official written transcript of a legal proceeding

trier of fact   the decision maker(s) charged with determining whether the necessary facts of a case have been proved—the jury in a jury trial, or the judge in a trial by judge alone

under oath   (in court) having sworn on the Bible to be truthful

unsworn testimony   testimony given without having sworn an oath or made a solemn affirmation

urinalysis   microscopic and/or chemical analysis of the composition of urine

voir dire   a hearing in the absence of the jury to consider the admissibility of a piece of evidence

weight   the probative value/importance assigned to a piece of evidence, based on an assessment of its reliability

wiretapping   the use of technological means to intercept (listen in on) private telephone conversations

witness   in a court case, any person who is called before the court to give evidence under oath or affirmation

worst-case scenario   an investigative hypothesis that involves basing one's research or actions on the initial assumption that the "worst case" (from the standpoint of legal responsibility) has occurred

References

Bennett, W.W., & Hess, K.M. (1998). *Criminal investigation* (5th ed.). Belmont, CA: West/Wadsworth.

Buckingham v. Daily News Ltd. [1956] 2 All ER 904 (CA).

Canada Evidence Act. RSC 1985, c. C-5.

Canadian Charter of Rights and Freedoms. Part I of the *Constitution Act, 1982*, RSC 1985, app. II, no. 44.

Chayko, G.M., Gulliver, E.D., & MacDougall, D.V. (1991). *Forensic evidence in Canada.* Aurora, ON: Canada Law Book.

Controlled Drugs and Substances Act. SC 1996, c. 19.

Cook, C.W. *A practical guide to the basics of physical evidence.* Springfield, IL: Charles C. Thomas.

Corbett, R v. (1988), 64 CR (3d) 1 (SCC).

Coroner's Act. RSO 1980, c. 93.

Cox, H.J. (1997). *Criminal evidence handbook.* Aurora, ON: Canada Law Book.

Criminal Code. RSC 1985, c. C-46, as amended.

Delisle, R. (1996). *Evidence: Principles and problems* (4th ed.). Scarborough, ON: Carswell.

Dyment, R v. [1988] 2 SCR 417; 45 CCC (3d) 244; 66 CR (3d) 348.

Gibson, J.L. (1998). *Criminal law evidence, practice and procedure* (looseleaf). Toronto: Carswell.

Hebert, R v. [1990] 2 SCR 151; 57 CCC (3d) 1; 77 CR (3d) 145.

Identification of Criminals Act. RSC 1985, c. I-1.

Jaffe, F.A. (1991). *A guide to pathological evidence.* Scarborough, ON: Carswell.

Khan, R v. [1990] 2 SCR 531.

Knowlton, R v. (1973), 10 CCC (2d) 377; 21 CRNS 344 (SCC).

McWilliams, P. (1984). *Canadian criminal evidence* (2nd ed.). Aurora, ON: Canada Law Book.

Olmstead v. United States. 277 US 438 (1928).

Paciocco, D. (1996). *The law of evidence*. Concord, ON: Irwin Law.

Rodrigues, G. (1998). *The police officer's manual* (15th ed.). Toronto: Carswell.

Royal Canadian Mounted Police. (1998). http://www.rcmp-grc.gc.ca/html/rcmp2.htm.

Salhany, R. (1991). *The police manual of arrest, seizure, and interrogation* (5th ed.). Scarborough, ON: Carswell.

Salhany, R. (1996). *The practical guide to evidence in criminal cases* (4th ed.). Scarborough, ON: Carswell.